HELD AT A DISTANCE

Held at a Distance

MY REDISCOVERY OF ETHIOPIA

Rebecca G. Haile

Academy Chicago Publishers

Published in 2007 by
Academy Chicago Publishers
363 West Erie Street
Chicago, Illinois 60610

© 2007 Rebecca G. Haile

Cover photograph by Steve Ladner

Library of Congress Cataloging-in-Publication Data
on file with the publisher.

*To my children and their cousins,
who will decide for themselves how to
define their relationship to Ethiopia.*

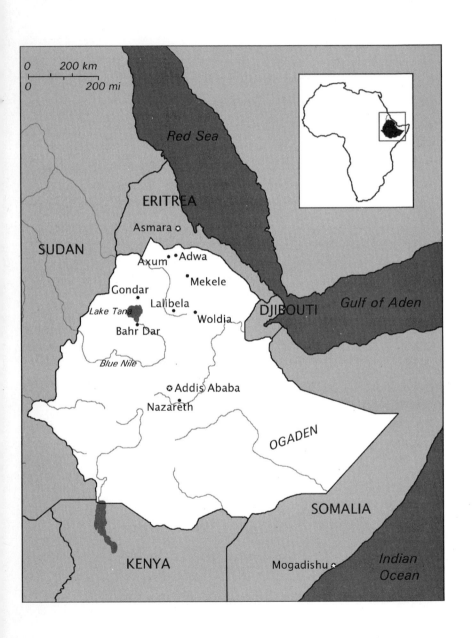

Contents

Held at a Distance

"I want the two of you to pack some clothes tonight because this weekend we're going to drive to Nazareth town to visit Ababa Haile and Temete. If we don't do that, we will probably take a plane to join your mother and father in America."

With those casual words, my aunt Mimi tried to prepare my sister Sossina and me to leave Ethiopia, even as she downplayed the voyage by equating it with a Sunday drive to my grandparents' home in the country. Mimi dared not promise us the trip to the United States, much less name a specific date. Those were unpredictable days in Ethiopia—days when people who disagreed with the regime didn't know whether they would see the sun rise the following morning, days when, my uncle Tadesse swore, you couldn't trust your own shadow. By then, government soldiers had nearly killed my father, and my parents had fled the country. How could my aunt and uncle assure us that no one would block our family's reunion?

Now, twenty-five years after those final tense days, I am on an overnight flight back to Addis Ababa. I am sitting next to my husband, Jean, staring restlessly out the window at the inky ground below. As we cross from eastern Sudan into northern Ethiopia, an hour or so before we are to land, the horizon finally begins to lighten. Soon, the sky over the vast highland plateau is awash in a deep, clay red. Jetlagged and on edge, uncertain what to expect from the country I am not sure I can still call home, I am grateful for this beautiful prologue to the month that lies ahead.

I left Ethiopia in 1976, two years after the army deposed Emperor Haile Selassie and sent a powerful wave of turmoil and state-sponsored violence crashing across the country. Along with countless others, my parents were swept up in that wave and soon the life they had built together had been completely washed away. In the summer of 1976, my parents, my sisters and I found ourselves abruptly deposited in the United States, stripped of our possessions and expectations and left to start over financially, professionally and emotionally. I was ten when it became clear we could not stay in Addis Ababa, and had just turned eleven when my sisters and I reunited with our parents in a small central Minnesota town. That first summer, as we watched our host country celebrate its bicentennial birthday with fireworks and cheers of freedom along the banks of the Mississippi, not one of us imagined how long it would be before we would see Ethiopia again. When I returned in the spring of 2001, I was the first in my family to do so.

The military coup that triggered our departure, and dramatically altered Ethiopia's political landscape, followed years of economic hardship and political volatility capped by the devastating famine of the late 1960s. Emperor Haile Selassie, who by the time of the coup had been king for over forty years, was perceived by many as out of touch with the suffering of his rural subjects, while his government was seen as more concerned with covering up the famine than with alleviating it. The emperor's apparent lack of empathy and his government's failures were exploited by his opponents, who famously spliced BBC footage of starving peasants and wasted farmland with older images of Haile Selassie attending lavish palace ceremonies and hand-feeding pet dogs and leopards. The doctored film helped turn a shocked public against the emperor and paved the way for the army's final blow. By September of 1974, Haile Selassie had been deposed, and an ancient African kingdom had reached a pivotal juncture.

That the coup would ultimately devastate the country was not evident at the outset. Many Ethiopians—university professors and students, union leaders and advocates for landless peasant farmers—longed to see Ethiopia evolve from feudal monarchy to socialist democracy. Advocates of reform worried about the military's power, but still hoped the coup would be a catalyst for the progress they sought. Within a few short months, however, all such hopes had been hijacked by a ruthless group of junior officers known as the Derg. Under the direction of the brutal Colonel Mengistu Haile-Mariam, the Derg imposed a form of autocratic rule cloaked in communist ideology. The new government soon began to harass, imprison and then kill outright those who disagreed with its policies or questioned its grip on power. Foreigners began to pack up and leave, followed by nationals who had the resources to do so. We were among the first to go, but our departure was just one step in what became a steady march out of Ethiopia.

On the eve of these dramatic events, my family had felt settled in Addis Ababa. My father, Getatchew Haile, who was born and raised in the Shoa countryside, overcame his poor rural roots by entering the country's religious school system, where he excelled and went on to win state scholarships to study abroad. In the 1950s he earned bachelor's degrees from the Coptic Theological College and the American University in Egypt and then a doctorate in Semitic philology from Tübingen University in Germany. After eleven years abroad, he returned to Addis Ababa in 1962. He was just thirty years old, eager to begin building his personal and professional life, and to play his part in the broader project of developing a modern Ethiopia. He began teaching at Haile Selassie I (now Addis Ababa) University, and in 1965 was appointed head of the University's Department of Ethiopian Languages and Literature. Outside the university, he was closely involved with the Ethiopian Orthodox Church, the largest church in Ethiopia, eventually becoming a confidante of the Patriarch (the head of the Church) and serving as the Church's representative to the World Council of Churches. He also became involved in politics, aligning himself with those who wanted Ethiopia to become a liberal socialist democracy. My mother, Misrak Amare, the daughter of an old Addis Ababa family, dropped out of the university in 1964 to marry my father and start a family; within two years, my younger sister Sossina and I were born. At the time of the coup, my mother worked as a secretary in the local office of Oxford University Press.

In the months just before and after the coup, my parents continued to pursue their personal and professional lives. In 1974, my father was elected to represent our province of Shoa in the Ethiopian Parliament, the post-coup civilian body the Derg tolerated for about a year. That same spring, my parents moved our family into a new house they had lovingly designed and built, and later that year, my second sister was born. For me, the period was a happy one. At the American school I attended, where I was in the sixth grade, the classwork was easy and my concerns quite mundane—how to respond to a playground snub, how to hide my crush on the tall American seventh grader whom everyone liked. Outside school, we were fortunate to have our extended family and most of our friends living within two hours' drive of Addis Ababa. We spent weekends and holidays with our grandparents, aunts, uncles and cousins. In short, we had the security and sense of well-being that come from close familial, social and professional bonds.

That security was shattered on October 4, 1975—seemingly a perfectly ordinary Saturday.

That evening, Mimi, my mother's sister, was to host a *mels*, literally a "homecoming," a party for a newlywed couple in the months following their wedding reception. In the morning, my mother, sister and I left our house for Mimi's so that my mother could help my aunt prepare for the evening and my sister and I could play with our cousins. My father planned to spend the day working at home and then join the party in the evening. With him in the house were my infant sister, our nanny and a groundskeeper.

At my aunt and uncle's spacious home, the day unfolded as expected, busy and joyful. The house was already brimming with people: my mother and aunts and older cousins gossiped and laughed their way through party preparations, while my sister and I ran around with younger cousins. I remember it as one of those perfect childhood afternoons filled with hours of carefree play and little adult interference. We floated frisbees across the compound, teased my aunt's tireless collie and her fat brown dachshund, shot marbles on the front verandah and speculated on how late we would stay up. But these games stopped short, though, when, in the late in the afternoon, we heard a sudden scream. I raced into the living room to find my mother, the telephone receiver in her hand, supported by my aunt and sobbing. Immediately, the celebratory mood in the house turned to anxiety and confusion. The caller, a friend and neighbor, reported that she had seen soldiers gathering near our house. She had heard shots, and was afraid that my father was in danger. Frantic calls to our house went unanswered and calls to other friends in the area proved equally fruitless. My mother, Mimi and Tadesse jumped into a car and drove across town to investigate.

Guests began to arrive for the *mels*, and those who did not immediately turn around and leave the house, huddled in close, quiet groups. Amidst the worried faces and hushed conversations, I felt small and unmoored, as if I were drifting alone along a slow-moving stream of stunned family and friends. I don't remember speaking to anyone, nor do I remember anyone comforting me or telling me what to do. I understood that something terrible might have happened, but I tried not to imagine it. Instead, I concentrated on willing each car that came through the compound gates to be our white Renault, with my father safely at its wheel. My parents had given me my first watch a few days earlier, and what I remember most about that evening is pacing the compound under a bright Addis Ababa moon, counting minutes, and then hours, learning an early lesson about the endlessness of time spent waiting, fighting back fear.

We never went home again. Not that night, not ever. My mother, aunt and uncle could not find my father or get concrete news of his whereabouts. When they reached our neighborhood, they found that soldiers—most just teenagers, many reeking of alcohol—had blocked the dead-end road leading to our house. They were shocked to see so many uniformed men and tanks on our normally quiet residential street, and my mother pleaded for permission to enter the house and speak to my father. The soldiers refused, and instead ordered her arrest and interrogation. The three of them returned very late, frustrated and distraught.

Over the next few days, while we camped out in borrowed clothes and makeshift quarters, my mother and family members contacted every person they knew, leaned upon every relative and every childhood friend they had, called in every chit they were ever owed. Finally, we learned that the Derg had sent soldiers to arrest my father and that he, fearful for his life, had refused to submit and had instead barricaded himself inside the house with a gun. His fear was warranted—at that time, people taken into custody often simply disappeared. In the gunfight that followed, he had been shot, and had been taken to a military hospital.

Several days later, with the help of family contacts, my mother obtained permission to visit my father at the hospital. The military refused to allow anyone to accompany her, so she was forced to navigate the long hallways of the cold, imposing building alone, passing through the various checkpoints, repeatedly presenting her papers and submitting to multiple searches. My mother is an intensely proud woman, and I wince to think how she must have bristled at the way those young revolutionary soldiers, intoxicated with their newly acquired power, behaved as she tried to pass them with her dignity intact. She got through, though, even managing to hang on to the containers of *injera* and *wat* and the toiletries she hoped to give my father. At the last checkpoint, she was pointed in his direction, and she hurried down the hall, heart pounding, dreading to see his condition. But just as she neared the foot of his bed, the soldier standing guard shouted at her to turn back. My mother protested that she had permission to be there, and my father, suddenly seeing her before him, cried out her name. Please, he begged the guard, let me at least touch her hand. I just want to touch my wife's hand. To no avail: although my mother had come so far, this last soldier turned her away before she and my father could exchange a single word or the briefest touch.

But my father had seen her, and seeing her had a powerful effect on him. As we learned later, the bullet that had ripped through his chest had missed his heart by a fraction of a centimeter but had scraped hard against his spine, leaving him paralyzed from the waist down. He had spent days drifting in and out of consciousness, unable to move his legs and unsure how badly he was hurt. He had no idea why the soldiers had come for him or what the Derg now intended, and was completely without news of friends or family. In the hospital, he had been surrounded by ugliness and filth and assaulted by the jeering hostility of the soldiers, mitigated only by the kindness of two nurses who had been high school classmates of my mother's. His grasp on life was so tenuous that the guards in his ward had placed bets on whether he or the man in the next bed would be the first to die; those who bet against him lost a few *birr* when his ailing neighbor died on the morning of my mother's visit. As my father tells it, in this, his lowest, loneliest moment, the sight of my mother at the foot of his bed was a sudden vision of beauty and grace, a heaven-sent flash of light and an unmistakable message of hope. ("She was only thirty then, you know," he says, whenever he tells me this story. "She was so beautiful.") The sight of her jolted him back to himself, and renewed his will to survive.

It took a long time for my parents to piece together why the Derg had targeted my father, and even longer before my father would tell his children about that afternoon as he experienced it. In the short term, once my mother knew that my father was alive, she focused on their immediate next steps, specifically my father's need for decent medical attention. Again, she turned to their network of friends. Thanks to his service on the World Council of Churches, as well as his university connections, my father had many contacts outside Ethiopia. These friends and colleagues helped bring the story of his arrest to the international press, and as a result he was transferred to Addis Ababa's Black Lion Hospital, at that time considered the best hospital in East Africa.

My sister and I were allowed to visit him at the Black Lion, the first time we'd seen him since the morning of the *mels*. Mimi led us down clean, quiet corridors past nurses in crisp uniforms, right up to a door guarded by a menacing soldier in full camouflage uniform and heavy dark boots. ("That soldier still out there?" my father would say, trying to lighten a visitor's spirits, "Someone should tell him I can't move my legs, so I probably won't escape today.") Mimi threw the soldier a disdainful look, told us not to be afraid, and sent us in one at a time. But I was afraid, and not just of the soldier. Inside the sterile white room I froze in front of my bandaged, immobile father. The idea that my father—the six-foot tall, laughing, in-command forty-year old in whom I'd never detected any weakness—was the man in the bed—that idea was overwhelming. I hadn't cried the night he was hurt, and I didn't cry at any other point before we left. But at that moment I could not hold back the sobs. I don't remember whether I even managed to say anything to him before I was whisked out of the room.

My parents soon decided that even the Black Lion was not equipped to treat my father's spinal injury. They then sought and, incredibly, received permission to travel to England for medical treatment. To this day, they are not certain why the Derg let them leave, given what its soldiers had just done to my father. The international pressure must have helped, and my parents certainly benefited from the fact that Mengistu was not yet fully in control, so that others within the Derg still had authority and leeway to make their own decisions. It is a sad footnote to this part of the story (though a central element of another family's story), that the official who helped my parents get their exit papers was later killed in one of Mengistu's many purges.

Within a month after the shooting, my parents were gone. They left me and my two sisters with Mimi and Tadesse and took with them only the most essential personal items. Everything else—valuables, clothing, pictures—everything they did not absolutely need, they simply abandoned. Indeed, the last thing my mother did in preparation for the journey was to cut short her hair—the beautiful, waist-length hair we used to beg her to let down. It was, she said with a dismissive wave, too much to bother with from now on.

Ethiopia is not a country where adults fret over children's feelings, and so my sister and I were left to cope with my parents' departure by ourselves. My aunt and uncle tried to keep us to a normal routine of school and home, but nothing could shield the two of us from the anxiety that gripped the entire city. Fear accompanied me to school, where a classmate mourned the death of his father, the last imperial prime minister, whom Mengistu killed one night along with sixty other prominent officials. Loss pulled up a chair at my grandmother's table, where family gatherings were now marked by absences—first my parents, then my closest cousins, who left after their father scrambled to find a teaching post abroad, then older cousins sent off on *zemecha*, a Derg program that conscripted urban youth to work in rural projects. And uncertainty dictated new rules of conversation at home, so that people were quick to exchange word of the latest crises and curfews but never, ever, spoke of my parents' return to Addis Ababa. For eight long months, I watched these events unfold and I held my breath, though I could not have said for whom or for what I was waiting.

In England, my parents spent their days in physical therapy and their nights in worry and prayer. My father regained only partial control of his legs and has had to use wheelchairs ever since his injury, but in time his health stabilized enough for him to begin the hard work of adjusting to life as a paraplegic. It is still difficult for me to realize that he was only forty-two when he was paralyzed, just a bit older than I am now and so young to give up the joy and freedom of physical movement. His doctor and close friend Dr. Asrat Woldeyes (who later was also targeted for his political activism, though by the Derg's successor) helped him take the first figurative steps down this new road, repeating over and over again how much a man can do with heart, hands and mind. Once my parents accepted that Mengistu was not a temporary phenomenon, and that the repression in Ethiopia and the consequent danger to them were increasing, my father began to look for work abroad. After about six months, and once more with the help of friends and colleagues, he found a position as a cataloguer of Ethiopian manuscripts at St. John's University, a small Catholic university in central Minnesota.

Once safely in the United States, my parents immediately began trying to get us out of Ethiopia. The Derg did not target any other member of my family when it arrested my father, but the government rarely granted travel visas whenever it suspected, as in our case, that the applicants might not return to Ethiopia. It took a great deal of negotiation and outright pleading with both the Derg and the American

Embassy before my sisters and I were finally allowed to leave for the United States. That last weekend, as it became more likely that we were indeed going to America, Mimi took us on a round of family farewells that for me had the same hazy quality as the first days after my father was shot. And yet I have the clearest possible memory of my very last minutes in Ethiopia. I remember pausing at the top of the stairway before entering the Ethiopian Airlines jet to London, taking the time to stare hard at the terminal and runway and the mountains rising beyond, and consciously trying to burn the images into my memory. Despite my aunt's efforts to downplay the trip, I must have recognized its significance, must have understood that this departure was the moment I had been awaiting. The life I had known was drawing to a close, and the flight was the first leg of a new journey.

My parents clung to the hope that our stay in the U.S. would be short, but in the years that followed, the political situation in Ethiopia steadily worsened. State-sponsored violence peaked in the "Red Terror" of 1977 and 1978, when the Derg routinely jailed, tortured and killed anyone suspected of opposing its rule. Hundreds, and then thousands, of people fled the country; those who could not secure exit papers often undertook harrowing journeys on foot to seek the relative safety of neighboring Kenya or Sudan. To make matters worse, Ethiopia was soon caught up in global politics. Its historical friendship with the United States ended with the revolution, and when Ethiopia and Somalia clashed over the empty deserts of the Ogaden in the early 1980s, they both became pawns in the Cold War. The former Soviet Union provided arms to Ethiopia, and the United States supported the Mogadishu regime; the ensuing war saw two of the poorest countries on the planet suffer untold loss of life and the squandering of precious resources.

The Derg kept its iron grip on power for a full seventeen years, until 1991. In the spring of that year, rebel groups that had been fighting for greater autonomy for the northern Ethiopian provinces of Eritrea and Tigre defeated the Derg's army in those regions and then went on to wrest control of the entire country. Across Ethiopia and in immigrant communities around the world, Ethiopians rejoiced at the fall of the Derg and the exile of the hated Mengistu (who now lives in Zimbabwe, under the protection of that country's despotic leader). Sadly, however, renewed hopes for a democratic government soon faded. The new regime, which was born as the Tigre People's Liberation Front (the TPLF) and once in power was renamed the Ethiopian People's Revolutionary Democratic Front, was initially an improvement over Mengistu's Derg. But it too has stifled dissent, murdered citizens and done just as much as the Derg to accumulate and retain power for itself. Today, more than fifteen years later, the TPLF remains firmly in control.

Ethiopia's road over the last three decades has been extremely difficult. In addition to political repression and violence, its seventy-five million inhabitants have suffered from crippling economic mismanagement, rampant government corruption, and the enormous economic drain and social disruption of the war with Somalia and military campaigns in connection with civil wars. Nature, for its part, has been nearly as cruel as human actors, unleashing long, recurrent droughts over the Horn of Africa that, together with poor agricultural practices, have caused widespread famine, most notably in 1984. Eritrea finally seceded in 1993 with the blessing of the TPLF, in an arrangement that deprives a now-landlocked Ethiopia access to the Red Sea ports of Missewa and Assab. More recently, the TPLF has taken the country down a dan-

gerous new road by pushing ethnic-based politics and prefer-
ences that emphasize the differences among Ethiopia's tens of
linguistic and ethnic groups rather than a national identity. In
response to this endless run of misfortune, many Ethiopians,
especially the educated elite of Addis Ababa, have simply left.
Prior to 1970, Ethiopians living outside Ethiopia numbered
in the hundreds; most were students who eventually returned
home to put their newly-acquired skills to work in the service
of their country. Today, thousands live elsewhere in Africa,
in Europe and in North America. Washington, D.C., alone
is home to a community of over 100,000 Ethiopian immigrants, and to walk through the Adams Morgan neighborhood of the District is to pass a dozen restaurants with wistful
names like The Blue Nile, Awash (another important river),
Ghenet ("paradise") and Meskerem ("September," the month
that marks the end of the rainy season and the start of the
Ethiopian New Year). Even unlikely Minnesota, where for
years it seemed that ours was the only non-Scandinavian or
non-German family around, now has a significant Ethiopian
community, large enough to support restaurants, stores and
churches.

Ironically, our exile to the United States gave my family, by
contrast, the space and safety in which to recover our footing.
My parents worked hard to shelter us from their financial and
emotional stresses so that we could grow up as fairly ordinary
American kids and then teenagers. In time, my father was
able to restart his academic career, culminating in his winning a MacArthur "genius" grant in 1988 for his research on
ancient Ethiopian manuscripts. I navigated the intricacies of
a large public high school well enough to win a scholarship
to Williams College, then went on to graduate from Harvard
Law School, to clerk for a federal judge and work at large law

firms in Washington and New York. I met and married Jean, my non-Ethiopian husband. As the years went by, I became more and more consumed by my increasingly American life and less and less connected with an Ethiopia I soon stopped thinking of as "home." When I spoke of what had happened on that October day in 1975 and in the days and months that followed, I often felt as if I were describing events that had occurred in a city I had never known myself and that mattered to a girl with whom I was barely acquainted. In leaving Ethiopia, my family suffered a sudden, painful rupture; we were simply forced to go. I found it easiest to accept the loss, and to turn away from Ethiopia, which had turned us out, and toward America, which had taken us in.

My embrace of our new life was also impelled by my feeling of being outside the mainstream of Ethiopian society. Because my family had lived in the United States for two years in the early 1970s, Sossina and I speak English better than we speak Amharic. In Addis Ababa, we attended English-language schools and were far more "westernized" than most of our friends or cousins. Even my name is the English version of the Amharic "Ribka." Once my family settled in the United States permanently, my sense of being distanced from other Ethiopians intensified. Early on in Minnesota, we came in contact with no other minorities of any kind, much less other Ethiopians. Since my parents were worried about our adjustment to our new country and its schools, they never insisted that we speak Amharic at home. The preservation of Ethiopian culture was not a priority for them as it has become for the generation of Ethiopian immigrants that has arrived in the last decade. As a result, we spoke Amharic infrequently and adopted a classic assimilationist approach to coping with our dislocation: in a stark irony for my father, who has dedicated his life to the study of Ethiopian language and literature, my two younger siblings speak no Amharic at all.

By the time I left for college and then law school, the number of Ethiopian immigrants in the United States was starting to swell, with the concomitant development of Ethiopian community centers and support groups, organized primarily around newly established local churches. But despite my parents' own deep Christian faith and my father's ties to the Church, my parents had rarely taken us to church services even in Addis Ababa, and I did not feel comfortable in traditional Ethiopian circles, which can be conservative, hierarchical and sexist. At the same time, I did not feel entirely American: I never felt at ease with the fundamental lightheartedness of my classmates or shared the sense of self-control and invincibility that seemed to underlie it. I struck a balance in which I displayed an American face to the world while I nurtured a private identification with Ethiopia that I kept mostly to myself. Held at a distance by the intervening years, by language and by culture, I felt farther and farther removed from our life in Ethiopia.

Such matters of identity and distance, combined with more concrete concerns about safety, ease of travel and money, had kept me and others in my family from making even a short visit to Ethiopia. Now, as I prepared to make the journey back, I wondered what I would find and feel. Would I be an outsider relegated to the margins of a country I did not recognize? I worried that I would feel uncomfortable with, or even resentful of, traditional society, for its assumption of religious faith or for its restrictions on the freedom of women. And I wondered especially what it would mean to be in Ethiopia without my parents. My relationship with Ethiopia is largely derivative of and dependent on theirs; I know that I have been able to develop that private identification as Ethiopian because of my parents' decision—conscious or unconscious—to allow me and my siblings to claim whatever elements of the culture suited us, without insisting that we take on a fuller set of associations and obligations. Was I ready to find out whether this identity and sense of connection would hold up without the filter and shield of their presence?

In the end, unlike our departure from Ethiopia, no specific event triggered my decision to go back. I felt an adult's curiosity about the country where I was born, and that curiosity overrode my concerns about cultural distancing and physical safety. I had come to a point in my life where I wanted to see and experience the country I remembered, to test my childhood memories against the modern reality. I wanted to walk through the house my parents built, loved and lost and to wander across the university campus that had been my father's second home. I wanted to visit my grandmother, who still lives in the house where my mother was born and raised, and where my family had gathered countless times. I wanted to spend time with Mimi and Tadesse, who sheltered and cared for us at a time when we could not care for ourselves, and to see what it meant to stay and live and work in Addis Ababa when so many others have fled. And I wanted to travel to the great cities of the highland north, to explore with my husband the churches and palaces and ruins of Ethiopian history that my own family never had the opportunity to explore together.

In May of 2001, twenty-five years after my family was pushed out, the lure of the country that I knew first and fundamentally, pulled me back. I persuaded Jean and made plans and bought tickets and got on a plane, wondering all the while whether I could bridge the distance that separated me from my first home.

PART ONE

Addis Ababa

A Solid Foundation

I am a little disoriented as Jean and I work our way through Addis Ababa's tiny international airport. It is 6:30 A.M., we haven't slept at all on the overnight flight from Europe, and the armed soldiers at every exit make me nervous. Our fellow arrivals are mostly Ethiopian, so I follow their lead through passport check and customs. When we are questioned, I suppress a prick of fear and listen to myself stumble over my first, tentative Amharic phrases. We get the extra questions because we are American, and the long looks, but we aren't delayed. Moments later we are outside, almost too quickly, I think, as I squint in the early sunlight at a waiting crowd pressed up against a metal barricade across the street. Then I spot Mimi among them, shouting my name and waving a bouquet of flowers, and my heart leaps. I squeeze past a cluster of porters and taxi drivers and into her arms, and suddenly I am wide awake and aware that I am, finally, back in Ethiopia.

We greet each other in a torrent of words and affection. My aunt has met Jean before, on her last trip to the States, and her embrace sweeps him in as well. Soon the two of us are in her car for the short drive home, and from the front passenger's seat I greedily take in my first sights and sounds of Addis Ababa. At that early hour the highland air is cool, scented with the clean smell of eucalyptus leaves, and the sky is a fresh, uniform blue. It is Sunday, and the airport is relatively quiet, but outside the gates we turn on to a four-lane road that is surprisingly busy with cars of every make, and aging blue-and-white minibuses bursting with passengers. There are no sidewalks to speak of, so pedestrians—Sunday churchgoers in traditional dress, urbanites in smart Western clothing, beggars shrouded in graying rags—hug the sides of the road to dodge the steady traffic. Cars and people in turn maneuver around livestock—donkeys, sheep, goats and cattle that sometimes come to a complete stop right in the roadway. Both sides of the road are lined with a disorderly mix of businesses, nondescript apartment buildings, cafes (including one literally shaped like an airplane), restaurants and untended vacant lots where eucalyptus trees spring up in uneven groves, and bougainvilleas burst forth with vivid splashes of magenta. Large billboards feature exquisite women and smaller hand-lettered signs advertise products and services from Coca-Cola to car washes in Amharic, English, and occasionally, Orominya. The city's bustle surrounds us until the moment Mimi turns into the walled complex where she and Tadesse now live.

Addis Ababa, this first drive reminds me, is not a city of public places. The Ethiopian capital does not boast pretty plazas, palaces or civic buildings designed by architects and urban planners; it is not a place where residents habitually stroll through public gardens or tree-lined avenues after the evening meal. Addis Ababa is a city of hidden sanctuaries, a chaotic and rather unattractive jumble that does not speak openly of the warm homes and other oases concealed behind tall compound walls.

I am not surprised by this reminder, because at the very heart of my memories of Ethiopia is just such an oasis: the solid, two-story granite home my parents built in Addis Ababa on the eve of the revolution.

* * *

Our house in Addis Ababa. Had events turned out differently, perhaps that house would not mean so much to me. It would still be important, but for the usual reasons homes matter: as a site of family pleasures, of cherished childhood memories, of private refuge from the city outside. But our house was also the place my mother, sister and I left one ordinary morning unaware that we would not return—and the scene, later that day, of my father's violent arrest and near-death. The juxtaposition was stark, yet I have always cherished the memory of our house as a private bulwark against the rootlessness and poverty that we suffered from after we left. Over the years, I'd let myself believe that something of the hopes and dreams poured into the house's foundations and built into its walls had survived the horror of that one day. Now that I was back in Addis Ababa, the house was the first place I wanted to visit.

My parents built our house soon after our return to Addis Ababa from my father's two-year sabbatical leave in the United States. Excited by their homecoming and ready to settle into a permanent home, my father and mother threw themselves into the construction of the first house they would own together. They rejected lots in newer suburbs outside town in favor of a parcel of land off the Sidist Kilo roundabout in an economically mixed neighborhood near the university. Once construction began, my father constantly swung by the site to check on the workers' progress. On weekends, or when it was his turn to drive our school car pool, he would take me and my sister and friends with him, a detour I loved for the fun of watching walls magically rise and rooms mysteriously take shape. He took an interest in the most minute details, frequently having workers redo this or retouch that and occasionally rolling up his sleeves to make sure every feature was precisely as he and my mother wanted. Back in Addis Ababa, one of my paternal aunts reminisced to me about how the workers had grumbled about his exacting standards. "It is as if," she had overheard one mason complain, "Getatchew believes he is building steps to heaven itself!"

As I think back on the years before the revolution, I see my parents, especially my father, as builders in a broader, more fundamental sense. In the late 1960s and early 1970s, the entire African continent was alive with the possibilities born of newly won freedom from colonial rule. Intellectuals like my father, many of whom had studied abroad, were full of hope for the modern, democratic and egalitarian nations they could construct through energetic, broad-based political action. They thought it natural for Ethiopia, the only African nation to have escaped colonization, to be at the vanguard of this new age of nation-building, and they welcomed the establishment of the Organization of African Unity's headquarters in Addis Ababa. The ideals of democracy, socialism, modernization and economic progress were very much on their minds (and pens); they believed that with hard work and collective action, these ideals could flourish in harmony with the traditional systems they still respected. Confident and optimistic, my parents were committed to building both a private home and a public society they expected to enjoy and participate in for years to come.

My parents' private efforts yielded a warm, comfortable home. Although we lived there for just over a year, at nine I was old enough to remember and take away with me a clear imprint of its proportions and beauty, the pleasure it gave us to be in it and the rhythm and texture of the days we spent there. I remember the delight of having so much space to play in and explore, in contrast to the two-bedroom faculty apartment we had just vacated. I remember the sharp smell of wet paint and freshly sanded woodwork and the exposed wires that dangled in sockets where we hadn't yet installed fixtures. I remember the bare dark earth of our new garden, and the tiny saplings that poked out of the ground into circles of protective wire mesh. I remember long games of marbles and jump rope and football during the single summer we spent there, and our many discoveries: a gutter to the left of the house that became, after a heavy rain, a perfect stream for racing paper boats; wood planks and pieces, left over from construction and stored in a basement, that doubled as seesaws, dueling swords and building blocks. I remember the time we spent with cousins who stayed for days at a time and the occasional grown-up parties my mother always let us stay up for.

I also remember, though with much less clarity, how life within our home was affected by the political situation outside the compound gates—the public project gone wrong. I don't remember the day Haile Selassie was deposed, nor the night Mengistu ordered the death of every imperial minister, but I do recall the hushed adult conversations, the curfews that sometimes stranded a late dinner guest on a couch until daybreak, the apprehension that seemed to weight the air. Yet none of this truly seeped through the protective barrier of our compound wall in a way that made me personally fearful. That is, of course, until the day we left the house, and did not return.

Soon after we left Addis Ababa, the Derg nationalized our house as part of a program of urban and rural land redistribution. The government decreed that each family could own only one residence, and it seized second homes, undeveloped urban lots and farmland property and leased them to renters and tenant farmers. Our house was our only residence, so its confiscation was illegal even under the Derg's own rules. But at that time my parents were in England, preoccupied with matters of basic survival and hardly in a position to protest.

The government kept and used the house for years. From time to time we heard scraps of information about its occupants: under the Derg, senior government officials, Cuban military personnel, East German doctors; and under the current government, more senior officials and then mostly foreigners working for NGOs. Once, maybe ten years after we'd left, a German professor who lived there with his family learned about my parents through mutual acquaintances and sent a snapshot of the house to us in Minnesota. The photograph showed the house framed by the garden, and we all gasped at the height of the trees, the little saplings we'd left behind. We should not have been surprised, since we'd been gone so long, but the photo was a sharp reminder of time and change in a singular place that, undisturbed by more current images, had stood perfectly still in our memories.

Two years before I made the trip back to Ethiopia, and long after I thought they'd given up on it, my parents won back their house. They hired a lawyer to challenge the original seizure, and ultimately prevailed, because the Derg had by then been overthrown by the TPLF and the new government was not as vested in defending the Derg's mistake. Once the house was back in my parents' names, Tadesse took over its care and maintenance. After some renovation and a few repairs, he and Mimi rented it to a British family affiliated with a local NGO.

That the house was ours again was important for me, too. Through the years of our unrooted immigrant life, for so many of which we were quite poor, the fact that we had been well-established in Addis Ababa sustained me at many levels, and the house was an important symbol of our former status. In our small town of Cold Spring, in central Minnesota, neighbors and classmates asked the most basic questions about Ethiopia, and I will always remember being asked whether we had houses where we came from, and whether those houses had glass windows. I saw myself as an ordinary kid—was I really so strange and alien to my classmates? Memories of our house helped me face my interlocutors and shrug off their questions. Since I was so young when we left, I had not yet developed a sophisticated public Ethiopian identity, and to the extent I had a sense of self, it was formed by my family and our life inside the private setting of our home. The memory of our house, of our private space, became the foundation of the Ethiopian identity I developed. As I grew older, I described Ethiopia as a proud African nation that had resisted European colonization, a country with an ancient history replete with literary and artistic achievement. This was the accomplished Ethiopia I let myself believe in, and central to this mental picture was an equally accomplished urban family who lived in a solid, well-built house.

I recognize now that this was a construct steeped in irony. For all of the positive sentiment I associated with the house, my father was nearly killed there, and "our" house was lost to us for years. Ethiopia escaped colonization, but it has been devastated by the brutality of its home-bred oppressors. Still, it meant a lot to me during difficult adolescent years in the

United States to believe that I and my family were rooted in something undeniably solid. Perhaps those roots weren't as strong and deep as my parents intended them to be, but they were vital enough to nourish and sustain me for years.

Back in Addis Ababa, I tell Mimi that I want to go to the house when the tenants are out. I want to walk slowly through each room, to study every corner while I mentally replay both firsthand memories and the stories I've heard from others. I do not want to be hurried and I do not want my experience to be filtered by the presence of anyone else with a claim to the house.

We plan the visit for late one weekday morning. We approach Sidist Kilo from the Arat Kilo roundabout to the south, following a wide avenue that runs through the university district. At Sidist Kilo, we make a right into the neighborhood, and I look for the house of a girl I used to car pool to school with, a classmate who many years later told me that she'd learned that bullets left arcs of red fire in a darkening sky the evening my father was shot. I can't find it, because once-vacant lots on either side of the street have been completely built up, but I do remember the route to our house. We take a quick left, past little residential shacks with corrugated tin roofs interspersed with the occasional larger home shielded, always, by stone walls and a guarded gate. About a quarter of a mile away from the house, we make another left, this time onto the familiar dead-end access road, the one the soldiers blocked the day of my father's arrest. After all these years, it is still unpaved and rutted. A few bumpy moments later we are in front of the compound, and Mimi leans on the horn. I am about to ask her whether the iron gate has always been painted a bright lime green when the *zebenya* throws it open and the house is there before us.

I climb slowly out of the car and stand in the courtyard for a minute, taking everything in from the outside. The physical look and layout of the house are exactly the same—given the years of state ownership, no one has bothered to change anything. But the grounds, by contrast, are unrecognizable. The lot was barren when we built the house, and we worked hard to seed grass, plant flowers of every kind (particularly roses, my mother's favorite), nurture tiny saplings and, behind the house, lay out a vegetable garden. Now, twenty-five years later, the gardens are simply beautiful. The small lawn is a lush velvet patch shaded by several leafy trees that look exactly right for climbing. Oversized primrose bushes and false banana trees hug the length of the compound wall, with long feathery branches that reach upward and then gracefully inward over the lawn. Everywhere, along borders, in terraced areas, in proper beds and terracotta pots, flowers are in riotous bloom, cradling the gray stone house in low bursts of color.

The gardens make me think of my mother, and how delighted she will be when I tell her that everything she planted has grown so ferociously, as if determined to honor her labor no matter what. They also make me think again of how time and nature do not stop for revolutions or pause to mark gun battles or mourn the departure of a family from its home. And then, almost immediately, I am much more emotional than I thought I would be, swept up in thought and memory about the solid granite house before me.

Without even closing my eyes, I can imagine the courtyard and garden crowded with angry soldiers, shouting curses and emptying their weapons as they search for my father. Years after we'd left Ethiopia, I asked my father what he had been planning that afternoon: trapped indoors, how did he hope to escape the soldiers who had overrun the compound? His idea—to the extent he had time to think at all—was to fight first and flee second. He thought he could fire enough bullets to keep the soldiers at bay until sunset. Once night had fallen, he hoped to steal out of a terrace on the west side of the house, climb over the compound wall and disappear into the neighborhood. And this was what he tried, except that the wall is high—built to stop intruders from climbing in—and a soldier spotted him as he tried to scramble over. I study the west wall and try to guess where exactly my father attempted his climb, then I can't help but see him lying crumpled in the mud below, not realizing at first how badly he'd been hurt, not knowing what next to expect.

I am shaken from my reverie by Jean, and the two of us walk around the house, to the east side, where the entrance is. Mimi is already inside with Qesela, a handyman who has worked for my extended family for years. He has come along to look at some water damage in the ceiling of the dining room. As we climb the front steps, Jean tells me that the house is not what he had expected.

"How so?" I ask.

"Well, it is big, solid, and the gardens are well kept. It's not what you think of when you think of Ethiopia."

"True—though you saw the neighborhood. This house isn't typical, at least not for this area. But come," I add grandly, "let me escort you around the family estate."

Jean, who first met me and Sossina when we were graduate students living on barley soup and ramen noodles, gives me a smile. He makes me stop so he can take my picture at the front door, and then we go in.

We begin with the upper floor, the main living space. To the left of the entry are the kitchen, dining area and living room, together in a semi-open floor plan. To the right, down a hallway, are the bedrooms and baths. In the living room, I am happy to see that the intricate olive-wood parquet floors that my parents painstakingly installed have held up beautifully, as has the big stone fireplace that still dominates the room. But everything else, of course, has changed. The neutral shades, dark wood furniture and Ethiopian and African decor my parents favored have been replaced with the British family's informal furnishings—a futon couch, scattered pillows, a silver-and-black compact stereo. Gone also is the upright piano that used to stand in a corner near sliding glass terrace doors. I realize, as my eyes move to that corner of the room, that I actually expect to see the piano there.

"Did I tell you that Sossina and I came back here once—and only once—after that Saturday?" I say to Jean. "Tadesse had the place cleaned up first, so we wouldn't see the mess, then Mimi brought us so that we could pick up a few clothes or whatever other little things we could find. I don't really remember what the house looked like when we came back, like whether the furniture was in place or gone, things like that. I think Mimi rushed us in and out. But I do remember our piano, which used to be there, in that corner. It was intact, but the panel facing the terrace was completely covered with these perfect little holes—bullet holes. They looked like they'd been made by one of those three-hole punchers. I'd expected the bullets would just tear the wood up."

We stare at the corner for a minute, as if a piano might suddenly materialize, bullet holes and all. "The soldiers probably had no idea what they were doing," Jean says.

"Maybe not. Some of them were just teenagers. Somebody told my dad that the soldiers retrieved thousands of spent bullets."

I turn around and start down the wood-paneled hallway to the bedrooms.

"Was there any one thing you really wanted to retrieve? When you came back?" Jean asks as he follows me. I stop and give him a look, because I know he thinks that I am not properly attached to my belongings, or things in general, and that he attributes this detachment to the way that we left Ethiopia.

"No—or at least I don't remember wanting anything," I answer truthfully. "I probably got some of my books. All I did back then was read. Oh—we did rescue our dog. We had a Chihuahua, of all crazy breeds. We found her cowering outside somewhere."

We pause in the doorway of the bedroom to the left, the one that had first been Mimi's before she left our house to marry Tadesse, and had then been my infant sister's nursery.

"That's the way my dad tried to escape," I say, pointing to the sliding glass doors on the west wall. "*Tye* Anjabu, too."

Anjabu is a distant cousin of my father's, the woman my parents hired to help care for us when we moved into this house. When the shooting started, my father had instructed her to stay inside a windowless bathroom with my little sister. But at some point he overheard the soldiers talking about demolishing the entire house, and he decided that they had to get out.

We cross the room and push open the terrace door. Jean steps out and leans over the metal railing. "She jumped to those steps from here? With a baby strapped to her back?" he asks. It is a distance of five or six feet, and the stairs are made of the same unyielding granite as the house.

"Yes. She didn't have a choice. She was afraid she would get hit by a bullet if she came out the front door. She bruised a knee pretty badly, but she made it."

As Anjabu later told us, once she was on the ground, she had crept along the compound wall toward the gate, uttering a prayer with every movement. When the soldiers discovered her they had been of two minds, some yelling that they should hold their fire, there was a woman with a baby, others threatening and shouting, in the language of the day, ugly insults about her affiliation with the corrupt bourgeoisie, not worthy of their deference at all. We were lucky—another aunt and uncle who did not know what was going on had just arrived at the house intending to pick up supplies for the party, and she reached them unharmed. Eventually, after they had captured my father, the soldiers permitted the four of them to leave.

We move on to the master bedroom, at the end of the hall, with its separate tiled bath and dressing area. After the soldiers had pulled my wounded father from the mud by the wall, dragged him across the stone courtyard and, as he tells it, literally swung him by his four limbs up and into the back of an army truck, they searched the house for the additional men they were sure were hiding inside. Furious to find that my father had held them off alone, they paused to kick and beat him for wasting their time and ammunition, then fell upon the house like vultures. Standing in my mother's dressing area, I can see the rapacious young men rifling through her clothing and jewelry and I try to imagine how she must have felt when she returned to her ransacked home. Even more than the loss of her belongings—though she resented that loss, especially the loss of an ornate gold cross she got as a wedding present and ordinarily wore each day, but had forgotten in the rush to get to my aunt's house—the violation of her privacy must have magnified her anguish and anger to an almost unbearable degree.

Along the east wall of the master bedroom is an intimate marble terrace overlooking a flowerbed where my parents liked to breakfast on weekends. Like the rest of the house, the terrace now holds other memories as well.

"That's where my father got that scar on his hand," I tell Jean.

"What scar?"

"I'm sure you've seen it. He's got a long scar that starts just below the palm of his right hand, and goes three or four inches below his wrist. He got it on that terrace. He told me that at one point he went out there to fire off a couple of shots. I don't know why. But when he tried to come back inside, he found that door locked behind him." I push at the door, and it swings open noiselessly.

"He couldn't stay out here," I continue, "because he was totally exposed. So, he says, he took the butt of his handgun and brought his hand down hard against that window pane there, the one next to the door." I raise my fist and pretend to bring it down against the glass. "He smashed the glass so that he could reach through to open the door from the inside."

It feels so strange, to stand on this terrace on a pretty weekday morning above a bed of beautiful plants a generation old and describe a scene of guns and glass and bloodied hands, even if my audience is Jean, who has heard most of this already. Strange because of the dissonance between the mundane beauty of the day and what I am describing, and strange because I have carried these stories and imagined these scenes for so long and now am finally on the stage where they actually took place. I can see Qesela poking at some bushes across the lawn; he gives me an exaggerated wave when he looks up and notices us there.

The entire house evokes strong memories and reactions, but only one room is truly painful to enter: my father's old library, the room that dominates the lower floor. The room has been stripped of its floor-to-ceiling shelves, and has long ago been emptied of my father's books and his inviting armchairs. The only thing the current tenants have put here is a wobbly green ping-pong table, perched improbably in the spot once occupied by my father's heavy desk. My father loved this room—he spent countless hours here surrounded by his books and papers. Standing in his library now, I can easily imagine him sitting at his desk, engrossed in an academic journal or poring over a newspaper detailing the latest political events. And then I see him on his final afternoon in this room, when the telephone rings. He puts down his pen and reaches for the receiver. "Hello?" he answers. Maybe he glances at his watch, to see whether it is time to finish up what he's doing and get ready for the party. "Professor Getatchew?" the caller asks. "Yes?" my father replies. "I would like to come see you," the caller says. "May I ask who is calling?" my father asks. But then the line goes dead, because the caller has only wanted to confirm Professor Getatchew's whereabouts before ordering the soldiers out of their barracks. "Hello?" my father tries once more before he shakes his head in mild irritation and places the receiver back in its cradle. He would have answered that call shortly before the soldiers closed in, and not long before he would be forced to relinquish whatever plans he might have had for his tomorrows. Did he have any inkling of what was about to happen? It saddens me to think that whoever now plays ping-pong in this room would have no knowledge of that ominous call, would know nothing of the events of that afternoon.

Walking back through the house once more, I try to memorize every feature, wanting to be ready to describe even the smallest details to my parents when I return home. Qesela goes on at great length about the work he and others have completed since the house was returned to our family ("Ribka, look at where we fixed underneath this staircase, the concrete was falling, little chips first then big ones, very bad. No, no—over here, on this side. Do you see that? And we made the storage area bigger, and then we waterproofed it—you must look at it, and you must tell your mother and father about that.") I can hardly concentrate on his words, but I understand that he means for me to know that the house and the grounds, and by extension my parents, are loved, cared for, thought of, remembered. Wandering the grounds, I again grow emotional with the knowledge that my parents will never live here again. I don't know whether they will ever even see this house again. They might never admire the aged sheen of their olive-wood floors, never nod with satisfaction at how well the masons' handiwork has withstood the years, never compare for themselves the astonishing new heights of their once-young saplings. For now, they will become reacquainted with their old home through photographs like the ones I will take back, brought briefly to life by my words as I point out details they will not find too trivial. My heart breaks all over again thinking about the distance between them and the house they built together.

That my parents were builders who were smitten by the possibilities and perhaps naïve about the pitfalls of the future, is symbolized rather neatly, I'd always thought, by one odd feature of the house: the steps linking the first and second floors of the house, beautiful wide steps of gray-streaked white marble, join the floors from the outside rather than the inside. This was a strange choice for Addis Ababa, where the midday summer rains can be torrential. On clear days, certainly, it was a pleasure to step outside for a moment when we moved between floors. But whenever it rained, we either waited it out where we were or risked a fall on the slick-wet steps in a dash to the other floor. I had sometimes imagined that external staircase as a sign that my parents didn't know the rules that builders must know, a warning that they were unprepared for the thunderstorms and turbulence that would consume the country.

Now, in the house again, I wonder: could my parents have done things differently, and thereby affected the course of events? That is, had they been less confident and more cautious, less idealistic and more distanced, might they have sensed what was in store and taken steps to protect themselves? Could they have built on the quieter, safer outskirts of town, perhaps, or could they have tried to leave Addis Ababa soon after the revolution, as others did? I don't think so. I don't think that my mother and father could have lived in anticipation of the devastation ahead. To do so would have been to live in fear and without faith in the promise of tomorrow, which is a far cry from the path they have always taken. I think my parents chose to build in Addis Ababa on the eve of the revolution (just as, a difficult decade later, they chose to build on the shores of peaceful Lake Kriegle in Minnesota) because they are believers, people of faith and hope. True, in one sense both their public and private projects were dramatic failures—the society they sought did not take root, and our warm, sturdy home did not protect us from the turmoil that rocked the city. Still, all of us enjoyed the house for the short time allowed us there, and for me at least the memories of those short months evolved into a powerful anchor against the rootlessness of the long years before we fully recovered our footing. My parents' faith and determination preserved the essence of their private project, and who am I to say that faith of such depth might not someday breathe life into the public project as well?

We have been walking around and snapping photos of every room from every possible angle for over two hours, and the *zebenya* and the maid have started to shoot us looks that suggest we have overstayed our welcome.

"Sweetheart," Mimi finally says, "Qesela is finished. We should go soon."

I'm in the master bedroom again, by the terrace. I don't want to leave. I don't much care if I am imposing. I feel a surge of possessiveness so strong it takes me by surprise: this is *my* house, I think, and I can stay here as long as I like. But my aunt is getting anxious, and I know that even Jean is ready to move on.

"Okay," I say reluctantly. "I'm ready. Maybe we can come back again, maybe next week?"

A minute later Mimi, Jean and I step out of the second floor and walk down the wide marble steps to the courtyard below where we have parked the car. At the very bottom of the staircase, I stumble just a little, but catch myself, and do not fall.

A Monday Afternoon

The last time I had seen my grandmother was at Dulles Airport in 1996. She was returning to Addis Ababa after several months in the United States and we had come to give her a proper immigrant sendoff: a long, drawn-out farewell attended by every relative living within reasonable reach of the airport (I had driven four hours from New York to spend three hours in the departure lounge) and replicated by the other Ethiopian families in the terminal. My grandmother was traveling alone, but she had not shown the slightest apprehension about the long flight ahead or been particularly emotional about her departure. Rather, she had been composed and serene as she sipped a cup of sweet coffee and smiled indulgently at a cousin who went on and on about the elderly Ethiopian man who had accidentally boarded a plane for Argentina the previous week. Her self-possession remained intact through our last embraces and farewell waves. Much later, I was hit by the obvious: she was leaving us, but she was going home.

My grandmother is the head of my extended maternal family, the many aunts, uncles and cousins among whom I was raised. Her modest house in Addis Ababa, her home for over seventy years, has always been the center of family gatherings. During our years in Ethiopia, my parents and sister and I spent nearly every Sunday at her house; we'd start with the midday meal she would prepare upon her return from morning services and stay on for hours of simple pleasures—family gossip, friendly banter, card-table gambling, children's games and laughter. When I think of my grandmother, that is how I picture her: surrounded by generations of family in the warmth of her home, presiding over an ordinary Sunday meal or a special holiday feast. Memories of those carefree afternoons are among my most enduring images of pre-revolutionary Ethiopia.

I don't regret having had to leave Ethiopia. To the contrary, I am deeply grateful for the safety and opportunities my family has found in the United States. I can't even categorically regret the circumstances of our departure, because I understand that had my father escaped unhurt that October day, the Derg would have targeted him again, with consequences that might have been worse for all of us. Still, I have always wondered what it would have been like to grow up in the Ethiopia we left behind, to come of age in a city we knew and where we were a part of an established web of family and friends. How would it have felt not to experience every single situation—the first day of school, the rules of dating, choosing a college, searching for work—as completely new, mysterious and daunting? What if, instead, I had had a reliable cultural compass with which to decode information and assess options? What if I could have made decisions as I have seen many American friends do, within the protective shield of family and with the myriad benefits that spring from roots sunk deep in one place? When I try to pinpoint the essence of what the revolution took from us, I think of the community and connectedness embedded in those Sunday afternoons.

As I planned my trip home, I wondered how much of this web of family and friends had survived the years, and how time now spent at my grandmother's home would compare with the memories I had so carefully preserved. Would the happiness and community we had enjoyed still be discernible in the place where it had flourished? Or had time and turmoil erased all its traces?

My grandmother lives in the Piazza neighborhood of Addis Ababa, in the center of town about fifteen minutes southwest from the university district where my family lived. Hers is a lively, diverse old neighborhood, anchored by the commercial strip of the Piazza shops on one hand and the venerable St. Giyorgis church on the other. Simple concrete and corrugated tin houses nudge the larger and sturdier homes of the well-to-do; and tucked among residences are cobblers, tailors and auto repair shops with wooden storefronts, along with shops selling everything from soft drinks and cigarettes to bundled eucalyptus branches for firewood. From early in the day to late each afternoon, the streets are alive with worshippers, market-goers, students, shoeshine boys and beggars crowding past cars and drivers and cows and their keepers. At one time, the neighborhood was also home to significant Armenian and Greek populations (my mother and aunts grew up playing with the Armenian girls who lived next door), many of them Piazza storeowners, but most of these families—who'd originally come to Ethiopia after the Russian revolution—left Ethiopia after 1974.

We went to see my grandmother at around midday on a Monday, to have lunch at her house. Not surprisingly, the changes wrought by time began with physical changes to her old neighborhood. Like other parts of the capital, the Piazza has been completely made over by the population explosion of the last two decades. The buildings were much closer together than I remembered, and groups of idle young men hung list-lessly around neighborhood alleys, another new development. The men weren't intimidating or hostile—I found that most Ethiopians remain remarkably polite and respectful of one another—but their youth and inactivity were signs of the unemployment and dislocation that have accompanied the growth in population.

Far more disturbing, however, were the scars of recent political violence that marred the surrounding streets. A few weeks before our trip, university students and the government had clashed over the presence of military police on campuses. The students had organized demonstrations to demand a civilian force; the government refused and ordered the students to stop the demonstrations. Tensions rose, and one afternoon government soldiers opened fire on a group of unarmed protesters, killing between forty and sixty students and injuring many more. In response, students and their supporters had poured off university grounds and discharged their anger and frustration at nearby public buildings and local businesses.

As Mimi rounded Arat Kilo and turned toward the Piazza, we saw that the flat, gray faces of the government buildings facing the roundabout had broken windows that gaped open like missing teeth. Shop fronts were smashed or boarded over, their display cases empty of the jewelry that should have been on sparkling display, and the main streets were strangely still for midday. The university, which was closed immediately after the shootings, remained shuttered during my entire stay in Addis Ababa. Persistent rumors of spontaneous demonstrations and swift police responses kept jittery city residents on edge—my family twice postponed the gathering at my grand-mother's for fear of the neighborhood's safety.

Past the commercial strip, Mimi turned into a warren of narrower alleys and maneuvered the car to my grandmother's compound. She greeted some boys she recognized while Jean and I banged on the wide iron gate until a servant unlatched the pedestrian door. Once inside the yard, with the door secured behind us, I felt as if I'd been invited to forget the damaged buildings of the Piazza, the boys loitering outside and the crowded neighborhood streets. I was inside another urban oasis, another urban retreat that I knew almost as well as our own house. I knew the dimensions of the yard from a thousand childhood games; I knew the angle of the slight slope from the gate down to the house from endless disputes over which football team or marble player had had an unfair advantage. I recognized the wide paving stones that led to the front door, and the graceful vines that climbed a weathered wooden trellis to the left. I wasn't surprised to see a tethered goat pulling at the tufts of grass between the stones, or to hear a dog barking from behind the house to announce our entry. I knew where I was, and the force of my recognition was nearly strong enough to carry me back in time to those lost Sunday afternoons.

Except for a fresh coat of paint, the single-story wood house was also unchanged. The front door, painted a glossy blue-green, opened into a large, deep-yellow room with matching blue-green interior doors and windows and dark floors polished from decades of domestic traffic. The front half of the room was a sitting area furnished with an old sofa and several mismatched chairs in an arrangement I knew by heart; the back half held my grandmother's dining table, six straight-backed wood chairs and a long, low hutch. A fireplace that I had never seen lit separated these two spaces. Its mantle and the wall above it were covered with old black-and-white photographs, including a beautiful shot of an aunt gravely accepting her university diploma from Emperor Haile Selassie, mixed with professional color portraits of grandchildren sent from abroad. An out-of-date calendar and an icon of the Virgin Mary shared space on the opposite wall. A door to the left led to a couple of bedrooms, and a door to the back led to the washroom, kitchen and the rooms used by the servants.

For a moment, I stood frozen in the middle of the room. Everything was familiar; my memories of my grandmother's house were fully vindicated. But I found that familiarity disconcerting, for how could the physical embodiment of a way of life have survived so well when, as I believed, that life had disappeared? How could this house be fresh and whole when, not five minutes away, so many other buildings were battered and broken?

My grandmother emerged from her bedroom a few moments later. She and I had already reunited at my aunt's home the day we arrived in Addis Ababa, so this time I could step back and marvel at how well she still looked. She was wearing the austere clothing she wears no matter where she goes: a dark, loose-fitting dress, a dark turban over her hair, sensible walking shoes and a traditional white *netela* over her shoulders. She must be nearly ninety years old (no one knows her exact age), but she remains mentally and physically strong and has lost none of the self-assurance that carries her through the busy streets of Addis Ababa or the cool terminals of far-flung airports. I like to think that her composure and self-confidence were forged early—she was married at the age of fourteen and had had six children before my grandfather died fifteen years later. Though barely thirty at the time she was widowed, and widely considered an exceptional beauty, she never remarried, choosing instead to raise her children alone on income from property inherited from her father and husband. For spiritual and emotional sustenance, she has had her faith, which is as significant to her as is her family. Church services, holidays and fasts define the rhythm of her days; for as long as I can remember, she has risen before dawn each day and walked the half mile or so from her home to attend morning services at St. Giyorgis. To me, she is a true matriarch: the mother of six children and grandmother and great-grandmother of many more, a fixture in her neighborhood and church community, independent and self-sufficient in nearly every way.

As we were the first to arrive, my grandmother put us to work arranging the buffet table and setting out the dishes. She had prepared exactly what I had known she would make: spicy *doro wat* and *siga wat*, chicken and beef stews simmered slowly in a sauce of onions mixed with chili pepper, cumin, turmeric and other spices; *alicha wat*, also a slow-cooked beef stew, but without the fiery pepper; *misir wat*, a delicate puree of red and yellow lentils flavored with a mix of spices; *gommen* and *atakilt*, dishes of mildly spiced spinach, collard greens, cabbage, potatoes and carrots; and, of course, lots of fresh *injera*, the sour flat dimpled bread made of *tef*, an indigenous highland grain, with which to eat it all. She had also baked bread, coarse warm squares flavored with fenugreek and anise, and roasted *kolo*, a snacking mixture of spiced barley seeds, chickpeas and other toasted grains. Though she herself eats very little, and has been a near vegetarian for years—this in a society that equates a lack of meat at a meal with poverty, or church-mandated fasting days—my grandmother is a wonderful cook. By the time the rest of my family arrived, her dining table was covered from end to end with an abundance of delicious traditional dishes.

I did not know all of the guests, but they all knew me, or had known me as a child and knew my parents well. Family and friends asked repeatedly about my family, wanting to hear over and again that we were all well, very well. Once past these opening assurances, the conversation lingered over the tender terrain of family stories, funny anecdotes and gentle queries. I met a man who'd gotten his first job with my father's help; another who had studied Amharic literature in his class at the university. I was reminded that my mother had been a serious troublemaker in high school, regularly lifting oranges and other delicacies from the lunch sacks of wealthier girls because she thought justice demanded the redistribution of such treats. Someone recounted the story of how at the age of three I'd refused to go home after my first week at nursery school because—as I apparently announced to my poor parents—I thought the house we were renting at the time a miserable barn by comparison; others teased me about the time my parents had pretended to put me out of the car after a quarrel with my sister and I had sat by the roadside and let the car drive off. I was surprised by how closely people I barely knew had followed our lives in the United States—they all knew I'd won a scholarship to college and attended law school (my grandmother even had copies of the small-town newspaper clippings)—and felt embarrassed by their outsized pride in our successes. And I was especially touched at how welcoming they were of Jean. They were thrilled to hear of his Greek and Armenian background ("Tell him the neighbors used to be Armenian! And we will take him to the Greek church before you leave—it is just right here, on the Piazza.") and went out of their way to compliment his skill with *injera* and to prepare him *gurshas*, choice morsels offered to a favored relative or honored guest.

Exchanging stories and laughter with relatives and family friends over a traditional meal in the old Piazza house, it was possible to go back for a moment to those Sunday afternoons, to imagine that not much had changed over the course of twenty-five years. The house was unchanged, the meal was the same and my grandmother was the same commanding matriarch I'd always known. Nearly every relative in Addis Ababa attended, even those who had to return to work for the afternoon. I did not feel at all the outsider I had feared I would be when I was planning the trip home: among family, in my grandmother's house, I felt embraced with an uncomplicated warmth that took in my *ferenji* husband as well. If anyone in my grandmother's living room felt any awkwardness born of time or distance or culture or language, they simply chose to ignore it in favor of expected familiarity and affection.

But of course a great deal *had* changed, starting with the difficulty in fixing a day for this modest gathering. The capital is now an unpredictable place, a city where people have difficulty with commitments of any kind. Even in planning the few weeks I spent in Ethiopia, everyone spoke as if no arrangement was ever definite and last-minute changes of plans were always expected. "*Igziyabher yakal; igziyabher ke fekede*—God only knows; God willing—you can never tell in this country," Mimi would repeat, perhaps just after we had made an appointment for the following day or maybe as we were making one of our frequent stops at petrol stations to purchase insurance against the gasoline shortage she feared could come at any time (her tank was never less than three-fourths full). That Jean and I had come to Ethiopia armed with several guidebooks—books!—filled with maps and tourist information, and thought that with good planning we could see everything we wanted during our short stay, was a source of infinite amusement to my entire family ("You want to see an *art* gallery? Here? And you think that this gallery is on so-and-so street, and that it will be open from 1:00 P.M. to 4:00 P.M., because it says so in your book? *Wey ye-ferenj neger!*").

And while my grandmother still lives in the house I remember so well, her yard is a small sanctuary amidst the crowded and scarred streets that I barely recognized. She will never give up her home, but most of my remaining Addis Ababa family, like other city residents who can afford it, have abandoned neighborhoods such as the Piazza in search of safer, less congested areas. Mimi and Tadesse, for example, who also lost their home to Derg nationalization, now live in a complex of about thirty houses inside a guarded compound in a suburb near the airport. Another uncle who had returned from the United States built a new house in a neighborhood so far on the outskirts of town ("Too far for there ever to be unrest, which is how I like it," as he put it) that he did not yet have proper water and electrical service, much less urban amenities like public transportation or shops. I understood these choices, but a part of me still mourned the diverse, vibrant neighborhoods I had known as a child.

And yes, my grandmother was her same unchanged self, but so many people were missing from her table, not least of all my parents. Until the moment of the revolution, my grandmother anchored a circle in which five of her six children (the sixth being a long-time resident of the U.S.) and all of her grandchildren lived within twenty minutes of her home, with scores of cousins and nephews and nieces close by as well. Today, only two of her six children still live in Addis Ababa. Eighteen of her twenty-one grandchildren, and eleven of her thirteen great-grandchildren, live in the U.S., in cities that include New York, Los Angeles and Denver. Many other cousins and nieces and nephews—almost every member of my generation—are also gone, living today in cities across Africa, Europe and the U.S.

Sitting in my grandmother's house, I thought especially of the high-roller uncles who used to be regulars at her card table, the ones who would tip me and my cousins outrageously for getting them a fresh beer or just standing next to them for good luck; the ones who excelled at the verbal jousting, banter and wordplay Amharic speakers adore. There would have been E—, who even before the revolution decided to fight for Eritrean secession, abandoning an aunt and two young cousins without warning; B—, the long-time mayor of Addis Ababa, whose body was found in low bushes off the Entoto mountain road, apparently murdered by a Derg official because B— took in a woman who had broken off an affair with that official; N—, a prominent lawyer and later in the course of his long legal career a judge on the Ethiopian High Court ("Above me, there is only God," he used to say)—whom I never knew as an adult though I too studied law— dead of liver cancer several years ago; M—, a university professor and human rights advocate who would have filled the room with his cigarette smoke, big personality and infectious laugh, at that very moment jailed on unsubstantiated charges of inciting the university riots; and many others, absent because they had long ago chosen or been forced to leave Addis Ababa or simply because with time comes change. I thought also of my father. Never much of a card player, he would have been relegated to an outer seat, and would have been deep in earnest corner conversation with M— or someone else, no doubt about Ethiopian politics and democracy's fledgling chances. And I thought also of the missing sound of children at play, of the shrieks and shouts that would, in the past, have been the musical accompaniment to any gathering in this house.

Lunch at my grandmother's house ended with one last echo of those Sunday afternoons. Dessert had come from Enrico's café, the Italian pastry shop near St. Giyorgis church, where years ago my parents had regularly purchased pizzas, cakes and cookies to add to my grandmother's traditional table. My aunt and I had stopped at the café earlier that morning, and although the place was sadly run-down, and although the owner despaired of the regulars who no longer came by for espressos and macchiatos, I was delighted that it was still in business. Enrico's was the only city establishment I remembered by name, and the café was as tangible a tie to memory as my grandmother's house. Now, on my aunt's cue, I blew out a single candle and cut the layered yellow cake we had selected, as if I were a child celebrating a birthday. The cake and pastries were as good as I remembered, and I savored this sweet taste of the past between sips of strong, hot, Ethiopian coffee.

I have always equated the changes wrought by the revolution with loss, an equation not easily recalibrated by a traditional gathering at my grandmother's house or several weeks among my remaining family in Ethiopia. Whether or not I have idealized them in memory, the simplicity and sheer fun of those Sunday afternoon gatherings are pleasures I will not know again, just as I will never know the other pieces and promises of the pre-revolutionary life I associate with my extended family. For my grandmother, however, anchored as she is in her faith, her neighborhood, her remaining family and in a way of being that predates the events that defined my Addis Ababa childhood, these same changes appear so much less fundamental. I have associated the life we lost most directly with her, and yet she has accepted our dispersal and carried on, maintaining her old home and keeping to her life-long habits. My grandmother's constancy and resilience thus open to me at least the possibility that my loss may not be as complete as I've imagined it to be. Pieces of that past remain in reach, vibrant and accessible.

* * *

My grandmother came to the airport to see me off when the time came for me to return to the United States. My plane was scheduled to leave at around ten in the evening, and I'd gone to her house the day before to say goodbye. We'd agreed then that she should not come to the airport the next night because of the long distance and the late hour. Independent-minded as ever, she hailed a taxi near her home and came anyway, sending a porter to find me in the crowded parking lot. She was sitting in the front seat of the cab when I came over, looking a little tired, but she made a point of getting out of the car in order to stand and say good-bye to me once again. I was touched that she'd come, and touched too by the topsy-turvy nature of the scene: here was my grandmother, matriarch of a clan now dispersed to the winds, out in the middle of a chilly night to see me off, a granddaughter she is content to know as her grandchild even if she does not know me as an individual and even though I have built a life far removed from her own. Later, as the plane cut through the night and I sat awake in the darkened cabin, hers was the figure I kept seeing, fixed this time against the swirl of harried travelers shouting at porters and shepherding luggage and bidding farewell to loved ones. I was alone, once again an American, hurtling through space by myself. But the image of my grandmother was proof, if I needed it, that my solitude did not mean I was without history and home.

The Engineer

"Your father," my uncle said, waving the book I had brought him, "and the other university professors—they are the ones responsible for the mess this country is in!" It was ten o'clock at night. As usual at the end of his long workday, Tadesse's thin, angular frame was stretched out on his bed. Hot tea and a light supper sat on his nightstand; his satellite television broadcast CNN International while we waited for the start of an English football match. The book he'd just flipped through was the *Bahra Hassab*, a treatise on the Ethiopian calendar that my father had published in the U.S. a few months earlier. The Ethiopian calendar is unrelated to the Gregorian calendar of the West, and many people find it hard to use. As part of his ongoing efforts to preserve and disseminate Ethiopian history and culture, my father had explained the correlation between the two calendars and prepared a chronology of important dates with rich commentary on the exploits of monarchs, the course of military campaigns and other historical events. He had drawn much of his material from Ge'ez primary sources, sources that few people can access because Ge'ez, like Latin, is the language of Ethiopian church liturgy and scholarly texts, but has not been spoken for centuries.

The book is an excellent new resource for anyone interested in Ethiopian culture and history, especially the history of the Christian highlanders.

My uncle was teasing me about my father, of course, but I also heard a serious note in his words. Tadesse *does* believe that the university professors and students who thirty years ago led widespread demands for political freedoms, land redistribution and a more egalitarian distribution of wealth, were naïve about the nature and limits of state power. Tadesse would welcome a representative government, but he thinks that regimes are nearly impossible to change and, once in place, inherently disposed to self-preservation. An engineer by training and an apolitical businessman by temperament, he prefers to ignore politics and fight instead for economic progress, specifically through the construction of infrastructure like roads, dams and factories. While my father believes that a nation is built with the bricks of political institutions held together by the mortar of national identity, Tadesse—who is as committed to Ethiopia as the most outspoken advocate of political reform—prefers the "real" bricks of infrastructure and the mortar of a free-market economy. For my uncle, the *Bahra Hassab* was proof that my father was still chasing impractical ideas—for how did decoding an antiquated indigenous calendar contribute to true progress in Ethiopia? Did the treatise create a single job? Could anyone drive a truckload of cement or spare parts down these highways of history?

Tadesse became a part of my family in early 1975, the year he married my aunt Mimi. Their wedding was a huge, boisterous celebration that must have been attended by half of Addis Ababa. It was the last major event attended by all of my extended family and friends, taking place as it did just before the revolution displaced so many. My aunt and uncle hadn't yet marked their first anniversary when my father was arrested, but Tadesse welcomed us with open arms and worked harder than anyone to deliver me and my sisters to our parents in the U.S. From childhood, I remembered my uncle as a benign, busy man who smelled of cigarettes and was warm and irreverent when he was with us. Now, back in Ethiopia, getting to know him as an adult was a pleasure.

Engineer Tadesse—the honorific is often employed in Ethiopia—is a man perpetually in motion. He is happiest when he is immersed in his work; conversely, he is impossibly uneasy when he is idle. Before this trip, I'd last seen him in Minnesota on Christmas Eve in 1995. He'd come to the U.S. reluctantly, for medical checkups, and stayed with us for exactly two days, even though we hadn't seen him in over ten years, and the next day was Christmas. On our first day in Addis Ababa, a Sunday, Tadesse decided to jumpstart our sightseeing and waved us into his battered blue Mercedes scarcely two hours after we'd landed. By noon, he had sped past every major neighborhood, church, palace and plaza in the city. After lunch, we were quite ready to surrender to jetlag, but he would not allow it: "You two have no time to waste!" he declared.

Back in his car, we ran a four-hour race through the countryside that took us from Addis Ababa south past the low-lying towns of Debre Zeit, Mojo and Nazareth until we finally reached the old resort of Sodere, known for its hot springs and outdoor pools. I had taken this particular drive many, many times as a child. I have cherished memories of rising before dawn to beat the day's heat and of Sossina and me bouncing in the backseat of our Renault, counting *tukuls* and donkeys along the way. Always, we would stop in Nazareth to see Ababa Haile and Temete in their dark two-room house with the tall papaya tree in the front yard. Then, on the final leg of the drive, we would hit a ridge from which the resort is suddenly visible, our cue to throw off our clothes and wriggle into bathing suits so that we would be ready to jump in a pool the minute we passed through the resort gates.

Like visiting our house or having lunch at my grandmother's, I had imagined that going to Sodere would be a pilgrimage of sorts, a trip I would make over the course of a long, thoughtful day. But with Tadesse at the wheel, there was no room for such sentimentality. His deep utilitarian vocabulary covered mountains, rivers, roads, reservoirs, buildings, factories and agricultural complexes, but did not encompass the unproductive realm of family experience or memory. On both drives, he actually stopped the car only once or twice, practically tapping his feet at the delay when he did. (At Sodere, where we drained the beers the owner pressed upon us in a quick half-hour, Tadesse summed the place up with: "Jean, here it is—the famous Sodere. I am sure she has told you all about it. Now you have seen it and you do not need to come back." On the Entoto mountain overpass, a beautiful spot high above Addis Ababa, where most tourists relax and enjoy the view, he barked: "Here. This is the best place to take a photograph of the city. Something to remember. From there— good. Now the two of you together. Okay, that is enough." For my uncle, lingering could well be the eighth deadly sin.)

For years Tadesse matched his appetite for activity with an appetite for hard living, especially during the periods he spent outside Addis Ababa inspecting roads at remote project sites. On that last trip to the United States, the doctors my aunt had begged him to see told him that his lifestyle was taking a ruinous toll on his health. My family is typically Ethiopian in its inability—or refusal—to speak directly about illness, so I know only that he quit smoking and drinking and began watching his diet, joking ruefully that living without ciga-rettes, beer and *kitfo* had reduced him to half a man. Maybe, but twice the worker, then, as the restlessness and drive that fueled those habits fed an even greater dedication to work. Now, he regularly spent twelve to fourteen hours a day in his office or on job sites, a schedule simply unheard of in Ethiopia (though much of what Tadesse does and says is quite strange for Ethiopia). Twice, my aunt cajoled him into joining us for dinner at local restaurants, but he could not sit through the entire evening. Both times, he begged her permission to leave after our plates were cleared, and while we drank coffee, he rushed off to check on his night shifts.

For most of his working life, Tadesse poured his energies into the construction company he founded with a partner in the early 1960s, shortly after his graduation from Addis Ababa Technical College. The company was one of the first private, locally-owned construction companies in Ethiopia. It eventually grew to be a big, profitable business that built a broad range of private projects and routinely won large public works contracts. The public projects included the tourist-class hotels in the northern towns of Axum, Lalibela and Gondar, which we would visit later in our stay, and roads in all parts of the country. At its peak, the company employed upwards of 2,000 people, making Tadesse a significant local employer and creating the circumstances that undoubtedly shaped his business and political views.

The Derg nationalized the company in 1978. One day, Tadesse and his partner found themselves simply locked out of their offices, replaced by men whose primary qualification for the job was party membership. We were gone by then, so we did not witness Tadesse's reaction firsthand, but I know that my uncle was devastated. According to my aunt, he was so bereft he could not work at all for several months. Eventually, however, his enterprising spirit must have resurfaced. He took advantage of Derg rules permitting the private ownership of small businesses and petitioned the government for use of a parcel of unoccupied land on the outskirts of town. First, he tried to establish a small construction company on the grounds. However, with his diminished resources and the uncertainty Derg policies had cast over the market, he could not raise enough capital to fund even the smallest projects. Ever determined, Tadesse tried his hand at unrelated ventures. He bought sheep and cattle from area farmers, one or two at a time, brought them to the compound to be raised and fattened, then resold them to urban households. He built a pen in one corner and persuaded my aunt to help him raise rabbits to sell to the expatriate community. (If I hadn't actually seen a forlorn rabbit's foot tacked to a wall the day I toured the compound, I would not have believed that he had dreamt up—and pursued—this particular idea.) He converted a ramshackle warehouse on the property into a woodworking and furniture workshop. For the next thirteen years, while the Derg remained in power, Tadesse juggled these small enterprises and opportunities.

Then, in 1991, the Derg fell, and Tadesse got his company back. The TPLF rebels who ousted the Derg favored Marxist economic policies during the early years of their struggle, including state ownership of large businesses. However, by the late 1980s they had begun to moderate these views, perhaps in response to broader global shifts away from communist and socialist models. In early 1991, just before their final advance upon Addis Ababa, TPLF leaders let it be known from their bases outside the city that, once in power, they would return several prominent businesses to their original owners. Tadesse's company was on the list, and the promise was kept. In the U.S., we celebrated the single best piece of news (after the fall of the Derg) to come out of Ethiopia since our departure.

The company buildings, located in a series of guarded compounds on a wide, muddy road about two miles from Tadesse and Mimi's home, were among the few places Tadesse stopped on our first day's whirlwind tour of the city. As he showed us around, his love of his work and his views on business were evident in nearly every comment. He skipped the administrative offices ("Just desks and papers, nothing to see there") and drove into a large storage and maintenance compound where he parked amidst a platoon of battered trucks and well-used heavy equipment. Here, surrounded by his earthmovers, backhoes and cranes, the busy engineer finally slowed down. He eagerly described the power and capabilities of each piece of equipment in detail, practically rhapsodizing over the subtleties of design, and opining on the quality of German versus American workmanship.

Not that he was sentimental about his business. Running a construction company in Ethiopia, Tadesse wanted us to understand, was hard work. He was hindered by poor infrastructure, incompetent or corrupt government agencies, a poorly trained workforce, too many employees more interested in handouts than hard work. Capital intensive projects posed special headaches. The machines he was so proud of were essential for certain heavy jobs, but they were difficult to purchase and maintain. It was hard for him to accumulate enough foreign currency to import the expensive machines from their foreign manufacturers. Once he had the equipment, he could not find enough mechanics trained to service or repair it, especially at worksites outside Addis Ababa. As a result, his machines broke down sooner and more often than expected, which translated into project delays and cost overruns.

Tadesse's solution to this last problem was to deploy manual labor—the most abundant and inexpensive resource available to him—in lieu of expensive machinery, wherever possible. The following week, when we toured a road the company was building outside the remote mountain town of Lalibela, we witnessed signs of both the problem and his solution. Here and there, we spotted machines abandoned in roadside gullies, awaiting repair or salvage, and we also passed two or three crews manually breaking up rock outcroppings and slowly clearing piles of debris.

I have always been intrigued by my uncle's atypical personality and views, and listening to him that afternoon and throughout our stay in Addis Ababa, I tried to distill his business and political ideology. Tadesse is self-avowedly agnostic when it comes to politics, suspicious of government in all forms. If he has an overarching political ideology, he is best described as libertarian in his social views and a firm believer in strong property rights as a foundation for economic prosperity. These views are consistent with his personal and professional experiences—he sees himself as an independent, self-made man who has managed to get by despite heavy interference from the state. As far as he is concerned, governments are almost always meddlesome and inefficient, especially the corrupt, self-promoting governments of poor countries. In this, Tadesse is right to differentiate himself from my father, who despite his personal experiences and losses, still believes that government—a democratic government—can be a positive force.

Yet despite his pro-business political views, Tadesse is not a typical businessman. True, he preaches independence and hard work and disdains handouts and government interference. At the same time, however, he is deeply concerned about the welfare of Ethiopia, particularly the problem of high unemployment and the lack of food self-sufficiency. While a businessman with similar concerns in the West might address these problems by lobbying his government or through private philanthropy, Tadesse thinks constantly about how he can craft his own personal and business decisions to promote that welfare. For example, when Tadesse got his construction company back in 1991, he did not dismantle or sell the small enterprises he had started during the Derg years. Instead, he handed these businesses over to friends and associates in need of work. Similarly, Tadesse prefers hiring people to purchasing machines, not just because labor is cheap and easily replaced, but also because Ethiopians are desperate for jobs. He knows that greater employment, especially among young men, means greater societal stability (as he dryly observed: "These young men with high school diplomas or even university degrees and no jobs and nothing to do all day—they could easily kill us all!") and feels that private companies have an obligation to work toward that greater good. In making decisions for his own businesses, therefore, Tadesse does not put first what is good for the bottom line over what is good for his employees and others affected by company actions.

These views had inspired my uncle to launch his most recent project—his marble business. Marble is plentiful in Ethiopia, and Tadesse decided there was a good domestic market (and perhaps, eventually, an export market) for marble tiles and slabs in residential and commercial construction. Quarrying the stone would require expensive equipment, but Tadesse knew he could design a processing plant that relied heavily on manual labor. The project thus satisfied his criteria for a good Ethiopian enterprise: it would utilize a locally available natural resource, it would require relatively low capital/foreign currency outlays and, most important, it would promote social welfare by creating new jobs. So he had purchased several tracts of promising land in western Ethiopia and built a processing plant just down the road from his company compounds.

Tadesse was consumed with his new project, and we accompanied him on several of his frequent trips to the worksite. The plant, housed inside a series of open, tin-roofed sheds, centered around several large and rather unsightly pieces of equipment that were loudly in operation on each of our visits. Few of these machines had been purchased new for the job they were performing. Rather, they were conglomerations of salvaged metal parts, rudimentary but functional, like the fifteen-foot vertical saw powered by a home-rigged water pump that screeched against the hunk of rough marble in its basin. I was taken aback by the dust and din and flying stone chips, but the twenty or so people I counted on each visit moved about with purpose and direction. In one area, a group of men strained to lift a piece of stone the size of an armchair into position against a circular saw, work that in a Western plant would have been done by cranes or conveyor belts. In a separate, quieter room where water drained off through ducts carved directly into the damp cement floor, workers hand-cut tiles while others honed the squares to a dull gleam. Finished tiles were wheelbarrowed load by load to an outdoor display area, where they were hand-sorted by size and color. We learned that Tadesse had begun running a night shift so that he could hire even more people, and that he made it a point to fill the lighter jobs with young, unskilled women who might otherwise have prostituted themselves on the city streets. The working conditions were raw, and Tadesse could not pay these employees more than 200 or 300 *birr* a month, the equivalent of 20 to 30 U.S. dollars. And yet nearly every day someone new came to the engineer to plead for work.

After the visits to his Addis Ababa worksites and our later tour of the massive Lalibela road project, I felt a bit in awe of my uncle. He had not only run (and restarted) his company in a difficult economic and political climate, but had found a way to accomplish social good through his projects. Tadesse was proud of the marble factory—proud of the self-sufficiency of his engineers and mechanics and especially proud that he had managed to create so many jobs, and he had every right to be proud. I could see why he touted his businessman's action over the endless prattle of intellectuals and political thinkers.

But for how long could Tadesse afford to conduct social welfare through the medium of his businesses? Could he really afford to be agnostic about politics when, as I saw it, his private companies and business decisions were so clearly affected by the political climate? At the most basic level, bad government means that many good companies are hindered by administrative corruption. The monarchy, the Derg, and now the TPLF, all favored businesses connected to people in power, so that the most successful companies in Ethiopia are rarely the best-run. Moreover, promoting societal stability or increasing employment are not matters a single businessman should or can tackle alone. Only governments can equitably spread the cost of solutions, and only representative governments are likely to craft those solutions to benefit as many people as possible, not just favored constituents. The problems that concern Tadesse remain entrenched precisely because Ethiopia's governments have not yet addressed them. Finally, even questions of national identity and culture can have an impact on business. For example, the current government's emphasis on regional and ethnic identity over national unity has created an environment where a contractor from Addis Ababa is not welcome in Axum or Mekele, no matter what his qualifications.

To my dismay, I witnessed plenty of evidence that Tadesse's businesses cannot remain competitive and profitable indefinitely in the current climate. His construction company pays the price of government corruption in the form of lucrative public contracts lost to well-connected competitors or in frustrating appearances before uncooperative bureaucracies. Both companies are hindered by the costs of Tadesse's social objectives. At the marble factory, for example, a manager we spoke to lamented the drawbacks of manual labor. He complained that consistency and quality were so difficult to maintain that he was forced to discard a great amount of finished product and could barely fill existing orders. The manager doubted he would ever meet the tight specifications of foreign buyers until he had mechanized cutters and other precision tools. For the same reasons, tiles imported from abroad were often of better quality at a comparable price. At the construction company, we learned that Tadesse was struggling to complete a road on which he had mistakenly underbid. Continued work on the project was damaging the company financially and straining his forty-year relationship with his partner, but Tadesse refused to walk away. His desire to complete another piece of badly needed infrastructure, his reluctance to dismiss the local people he'd hired and his own obstinate pride simply would not allow it. I loved my uncle for his determination, yet the potential for a catastrophe was plain. Tadesse's businesses could suffer, even unravel, leaving the people who depend on him out in the cold.

Tadesse, with his worthy social objectives and unorthodox solutions, needs political change as much as any Ethiopian.

* * *

Tadesse's drive to promote Ethiopian welfare did not stop with steps he could take with his own companies. Soon after our arrival in Addis Ababa, he handed us a thick bound document entitled "A Proposal for How to Eradicate Hunger in Ethiopia." The pragmatic businessman, it turned out, harbors his own grand dreams.

The chronic water shortages and related crop failures that keep Ethiopia poor are well known in the West. They are entrenched national problems that cry out for strong leadership and resolute collective action. Incredibly, Tadesse had decided to search for a solution himself. Following his instincts about the volume of water in Ethiopia's highland rivers, Tadesse studied the large regional rivers and their tributaries, poring over reams of route and flow-volume data from the Ministry of Water Resources and the Ethiopian Mapping Agency. He was now convinced that Ethiopia could in fact feed its people if only the government would commit itself to a solution. He had summarized his findings in his proposal and, admitting that a project of this scope needed government support, intended to present the document to the prime minister himself.

The premise of Tadesse's astonishing thesis was simple. First, there is more than enough water in the abundant rivers of Ethiopia's central highlands—particularly given the volume of increased flow during the three-month rainy season—to satisfy the country's agricultural needs. Currently, most of this water runs off during the saturated rainy season, sometimes washing away fertile soil. Second, because most of these rivers, including the Blue Nile and its tributaries, are at elevations higher than the country's agricultural areas, engineers could exploit the drop in elevation to collect their waters and route it towards lower-lying farmlands in a cost-efficient manner. Specifically, Tadesse pointed out that Lake Ziway, an existing crater lake near Addis Ababa, could be enlarged to create an enormous reservoir. Using the region's natural topography to maximum advantage, several rivers could be diverted or partly channeled so that their waters collected in the lower-elevation lake during the rainy season. The conserved water could then be released to farms whenever the rains failed or even to lengthen the growing season.

The proposal also anticipated huge collateral benefits. Water from the new reservoir could ease Addis Ababa's persistent water shortages, a serious urban problem. New dams could be built on untapped highland rivers—again capitalizing on natural elevation drops—to generate massive amounts of hydroelectric energy that could power development across the country. Finally, the project could create thousands of jobs as cheap labor could be deployed to do the work of redirecting river tributaries, expanding the reservoir and building the many kilometers of new irrigation canals.

In his salon/bedroom one evening, with CNN once again in the background, Tadesse pressed Jean and me on the proposal. "I want to know your opinion. Of course, it would be much better if Sossina were here. She is an engineer and she would understand what I am saying. But anyway tell me what you lawyers think." What I thought was that the document was pure Tadesse—part lecture decrying the national shame of famine and continued reliance on Western food aid, part enthusiastic discussion of ambitious engineering feats, and part pep talk about finding the national will to bring dramatic benefits to Ethiopia. Once again I felt in awe of my uncle—for his love of country, for his spirited solve-it-yourself approach and especially for his faith that his personal actions could spark a national response. Here was a man determined to do something. And, of course, I also thought—will this proposal ever make it to the prime minister's desk, much less come to fruition?

I didn't dare mention that last thought to Tadesse. Instead, we offered the help he'd asked for. We asked questions: what about environmental considerations? Who would buy the additional energy the dams would generate? How had he calculated costs?

We discussed style: why not cast his ambitious project as a series of smaller projects to give the prime minister manageable alternatives in case he or his advisors found the entire project too daunting? Why not rephrase the language of national pride and exhortation to action in order to spare the reader who did not agree with his every point? Tadesse cheerfully considered our observations, going over them with obvious enjoyment.

A little later, my aunt entered the room and chastised Tadesse for keeping us up late with "that proposal of yours." But I had enjoyed the discussion, and suddenly I wanted to help Tadesse move his project forward. So as we said our goodnights, I volunteered to rewrite the document. I told Tadesse that I could incorporate the suggestions he'd liked and polish the English and technical language to make it comprehensible to non-engineer readers like the prime minister and his staff. Ever a fan of work and people who work, and thinking, I am certain, that the three weeks I'd already spent in Ethiopia were more than enough leisure for any adult, Tadesse waved off my aunt's objections—"Let her use her big American brain!"—and enthusiastically accepted my offer.

A few days later, Zaynu, Tadesse's driver of many years, took me to the office, a neat horseshoe-shaped building that the Derg had built when it controlled the company. A smooth gravel driveway traced the interior of the horseshoe, and a circle of garden in the middle was bright with well-tended roses. Inside, large offices for senior engineers and managers lined the outer edge of the horseshoe, with smaller, shared offices along the interior for junior staff and assistants. Tadesse's secretary led me to one of these smaller offices and showed me to a computer. By 5 P.M., the offices had nearly cleared, and by the time the sun set at 6 P.M. there was no one around to distract me—except Zaynu. I had intended to stay until I completed the revision, but every twenty minutes he popped in to "see if I needed anything" until I felt I had to leave. The next day, I suggested that instead of Zaynu waiting around while I worked, my uncle should pick me up on his way home from checking on the marble factory night shift at around 10 P.M., as was his custom. My aunt, who had insisted that Zaynu stay with me the previous day, reluctantly conceded that I could manage a few hours alone inside a guarded office compound.

Once dropped off as planned, I quickly settled into the same office. Soon, I was completely absorbed in water levels, irrigation routes and inspirational rhetoric, and I made good progress for a couple of hours. Then, suddenly, without any warning at all, the power went out. My computer crashed and the screen went blank; every light in the room blinked off and I was in total darkness. I could not even discern the window from the wall around it, because the power outage had evidently cut a wide swathe through the neighborhood.

When the lights did not come back on, I called the house for help. Tadesse was out working and by rare chance my aunt too was out for the evening. Vaguely thinking that I would go in search of the compound guard, I poked my head out the office door, but the solid black wall of the hallway was even more disconcerting than the dark of the office. Flustered and at a complete loss, I retreated, locked the office door and sat on the edge of a chair by the open window.

I waited in total silence and darkness for about thirty minutes before Tadesse came to my rescue. I could tell that he was worried about me, but once he saw that I had not fallen completely apart, he immediately reverted to his teasing self.

"Aha!" he cried, waving his flashlight around the room. "Now you know! I am glad you have seen for yourself what it means to work in Ethiopia. You see how nothing is simple here. These are the problems we must deal with every day. And now you will also have a good story to tell your friends back in New York!" I think a part of him really was glad I'd experienced the outage like that. In any event, just as quickly as Tadesse's flashlight dispelled the dark, his usual good cheer and high energy restored my spirits.

I collected my things, wondering how much of my revision I had lost when the computer crashed, and I felt the irony of what I was doing. I had come to Tadesse's office to refine the text of an ambitious proposal for a huge public works project involving diverting rivers, blasting mountains and constructing miles of irrigation canals in a country that, for the moment, couldn't provide basic necessities like reliable electricity. Given the scope and depth of Ethiopia's problems, it seemed absurd for Tadesse to spend even five more minutes on the proposal. During our tour of Tadesse's Lalibela road, I learned that back in the eleventh century, the Emperor

Lalibela had also dreamt of diverting the waters of the Blue Nile to benefit his farmers. Was Tadesse's pursuit of this same dream eight centuries later so different from dreaming about democracy, or so much less romantic than reveling in the long history of the country's unique calendar?

But by then, of course, I knew that that was not the way Tadesse saw things. For my uncle, it is critical to keep building, to keep taking small, manageable steps, no matter how difficult the immediate circumstances or how utopian the ultimate goal. This dedicated, practical engineer moves from project to project, marking his progress in small but tangible economic notches. And if, as I suspected, this strategy was born in part to fight off despair about the possibility of greater gains—well, so be it. Work can also be an end in itself, as valuable as what it produces. A marble factory can be as much about Ethiopians having jobs as it is about creating beautiful tiles and generating profits, and an engineer's ambitious proposal can be as much about preserving hope as it is about immediate, concrete action. Tadesse was wrong to think he could remain agnostic about politics, but did that mean his strategy was bad for Ethiopia?

As for me, after three weeks of being around Tadesse, I must have come under his influence. Driving home through the darkened city streets, warmed by Tadesse's good-natured teasing, I didn't feel despondent about the project's chances. Rather, I felt gratified that through Tadesse I was making a small contribution to a proposal to benefit Ethiopia. When we were still students, my sister and I used to talk of someday returning to Ethiopia and performing some service, she as an engineer and I as a teacher of English or the law. In the end, I had come back as an ordinary tourist, so I found it gratifying to put my mind to work, if only for a few hours. Beyond that, it just felt good to help my uncle on a project that meant so much to him. I did not need to believe in the success of Tadesse's proposal to know that Ethiopia will never progress without the efforts of both its pragmatic builders and its political dreamers. I enjoyed putting aside my tiresome lawyer's habit of finding problems in every course of action to join him in his work. By the time we reached the house, I had mentally mapped out the sections I would revise the following day.

A few months later, my father forwarded a posting he'd seen on the internet reporting a speech my uncle had given to the Ethiopian Association of Engineers on his proposal. Reading through the report, I smiled to see that one of Tadesse's first slides declared, in big, bold letters: "If only [thirty years ago] we had made our slogan 'water for the tiller' instead of 'land for the tiller,' we would not be hungry today!"

PART TWO

The Historic North

Remains of an Empire

It was a little past 7 A.M., and the dusty streets of Axum were slowly coming to life. Schoolchildren in neat uniforms walked arm-in-arm while men and women unlocked storefronts, carried produce to market and drove livestock down the town's main avenue. *Garis*, open flatbed carts harnessed to horses or mules, clattered back and forth, ferrying passengers and hauling goods. Drivers and pedestrians exchanged greetings and shouted warnings in Tigrinya, the regional language. At the west end of town, Jean stopped to photograph a lone *gari* at an Agip petrol station. The driver had climbed down to fill a dented red jerry can with gasoline, and his mule stood right in front of the pump with its head and ears drooping in a line perpendicular to the dirt lot, creating an irresistibly funny picture. Past the Agip station, the town's morning bustle died down, and soon we were alone on the westward road toward Gondar. To the south stretched unbroken flat brown fields; to the north, hills dotted with trees and shrubs rose gently from the gravel road. Behind us, in the distance, we could just make out "King Ezana's" obelisk, piercing the sky over the town's low buildings.

My family left Ethiopia before I had a chance to visit any of the great historic sites of the north, and I was determined to get to all of them on this trip home. Each of these places—Lalibela, Gondar, Lake Tana and, above all, the city of Axum—represents an important piece of Ethiopian history. Lalibela is home to massive monolithic churches that eleventh century masons extracted from solid mountainsides; Lake Tana has atmospheric monasteries that depict multiple facets of an age-old Church; and in Gondar are medieval palaces where kings, courtiers and early Portuguese explorers plotted royal intrigues. Axum, the oldest and most important of these places, is also the hardest to categorize. As I would discover, the city is home to an extraordinary mix of ancient ruins, historic churches and present-day tensions that reveals a complex and unsettling picture of nation and national identity.

Two thousand years ago, Axum was at the center of an empire that stretched from northern Ethiopia across the Red Sea to the South Arabian peninsula. Several centuries later, Axum witnessed the birth of Ethiopian Christianity and the rise of powerful legends that linked Ethiopia's monarchs to Israel and laid claim to the Ark of the Covenant. Nineteenth-century Axum signified the line the colonial Italians could not cross—the town sits just south of Adwa, the famous battlefield where Emperor Menelik's ragtag army stunned the aggressors in 1896. Today Axum is the last town of any size before modern Ethiopia stops and the newly independent Eritrea begins; it is just a few miles south of the barren plains where the two countries fought a border war that lasted for two years. Axum thus encompasses three distinct strands of Ethiopian identity: ancient empire, Christian kingdom and divided modern nation.

My visit to Axum brought me face-to-face with these strands, and the experience left me feeling as though I had walked out of a theater before the final act. As the curtains parted, I saw a familiar and inspiring Ethiopia reflected in Axum's older sites and stories. The specific accomplishments of ancient Axum were new discoveries, but ones that fit with my preexisting idea of Ethiopia as a nation of stature and achievement. Christian Ethiopia was also familiar, known to me through my family's faith. But Ethiopia as a divided nation, reflected in the loss of Eritrea and the regionalism now afoot in Axum itself, was an altogether different matter. I did not recognize this last Ethiopia and I could not reconcile it with the national image I had always assumed.

Ancient Axum is symbolized best by the soaring stone obelisks, or stelae, for which the town is most famous. Jean and I hired a guide we met in front of the tiny National Museum, and headed straight for the Stelae Park, a field in the center of town protected by barbed wire and a solitary guard with a rifle slung across his shoulders. At one time, this field was home to six enormous and elaborately carved stelae—the tallest of them reaching an astonishing 33 meters, the heaviest weighing nearly 500 tons—as well as many smaller stones. The park still contains an impressive array of the stones, and, although we had seen photographs of the stelae in books and brochures, our reaction as we approached the site was disbelief. How on earth, we wondered, had the ancient Axumites managed to extract such large blocks of granite from quarries outside town and transport them intact to the park, a distance of over four kilometers? How had they then sunk the finished stones into pits deep enough and strong enough to hold them upright for centuries? The stelae were beautiful: the large stones are characterized by an intricate pattern of false doors and windows punctuated by rows of protruding knobs, known locally as "monkey heads." The Axumites' intention, our guide said, had been to invoke a contemporary multistory residence in which layers of flat stone would alternate with protruding wooden beams; the result, to my eye, was an aesthetic, spare geometry unlike anything I had ever seen.

The stelae are Axum's most dramatic ruins, but there are many other significant sites. These include a series of cavernous underground tombs built of precisely worked granite blocks, private residences such as the sixth-century Dungur palace, an exquisite ochre ruin on the outskirts of town with a sophisticated and still-visible drainage system, and public sites like Mai Shum, an enormous basin dug to collect runoff from two rivers that once ran through the now-arid town. Incredibly, archeologists believe that they have so far excavated less than two percent of Axum's archeologically important sites. Moreover, given Ethiopia's poverty, much of what has been excavated has not been fully studied or properly exhibited. One of our most remarkable stops was at a little wooden shed, no bigger than a telephone booth, that stood alone at the edge of a deserted field. Jean and I exchanged glances as our guide searched his pockets for the key to the padlocked door—what could possibly be stored in a shed? Answer: a priceless fourth-century granite slab inscribed in Ge'ez, Sabean and Greek. Emperor Ezana had commissioned the slab to thank God for military victories in Sudan, and it was a major discovery for what it revealed about the empire's strength, the language of its elite and the king's religious convictions. A farmer turning his fields had found the stone several years earlier, and incredibly, there it remained, as if it were no more precious than a rusty garden tool.

From excavated ruins, recovered artifacts and the accounts of the seafaring merchants, missionaries, envoys and enemies who came in contact with the kingdom, historians agree that a sophisticated civilization of antiquity once flourished in Axum.

The region's first settlements date from the fifth century B.C.; by the second century B.C. the kingdom stretched across the northern Ethiopian highlands to the low-lying areas of the Red Sea coast. In the fourth and fifth centuries, Axum expanded its dominion across the Red Sea and for brief periods actually controlled parts of the South Arabian peninsula. It established commercial and diplomatic contacts with the Roman and Byzantine empires, Mecca and even far-off India and Sri Lanka; its elite communicated in Greek, Sabean and Ge'ez. At home, its accomplishments were equally impressive. Axum developed the Ethiopic script, the script indigenous to Ethiopia. Its kings issued their own coinage, something few of their contemporaries had the wealth or status to do. Finally, as the stelae and other monuments testify, the Axumites were sophisticated architects, engineers and masons with a fine eye for the artistic.

Christian Axum exists on top of these ancient foundations, physically and psychologically. Its primary physical site is the St. Mary of Tsion church compound, located right across from the Stelae Park, where Emperor Ezana built the first Ethiopian cathedral after he converted to Christianity in the fourth century. Today, the compound is home to the current "old" St. Mary's, built on Ezana's original foundations by King Fasiledes of Gondar in 1655; the "new" St. Mary's, commissioned by Haile Selassie in the 1960s and, off within its own enclosure, the mysterious rectangular chapel that is said to house the Ark of the Covenant.

Christian Axum is also embodied in two foundational legends that are intertwined with early Axumite history. In the first, relating to the founding of the so-called Solomonic dynasty of rulers, the main Ethiopian protagonist is Makda, a queen of Axum, also known as the Queen of Sheba, who traveled to Jerusalem for an audience with the wise King Solomon, who welcomed the beautiful queen but soon tricked her into a tryst. He had made her promise that she would take nothing from his palace without his permission, then, after serving a spicy meal, left a carafe of water by her bed from which she drank when she awoke thirsty. As she had taken the water without his permission, he held her to her promise. The queen returned to Axum carrying the king's child, the future King Menelik I and the first of the royal Solomonic line.

The second legend describes how the Ark of the Covenant came to Ethiopia. According to this story, the adult Menelik traveled to Jerusalem to visit his father. King Solomon was pleased with his son, and selected a group of Levite men to aid him in his administration of Ethiopia. The Levites, the traditional guardians of the Ark, refused to leave Israel without it. They secretly removed the holy relic from the Temple in Jerusalem, and left for Axum with Menelik before Solomon discovered the loss.

These stories quickly became an integral part of Ethiopia's early Judeo-Christian identity. The country was glorified by these unique tales and its people were elevated by the message that they had inherited from Israel the mantle of God's chosen people. For their part, Ethiopian monarchs promoted the notion of the Solomonic dynasty with great success, thereby fortifying their claim to divine rule and reinforcing the symbiotic link between church and state. (The constitution drafted under Haile Selassie in 1955 literally states that Ethiopia's monarchs descended from King Solomon and the Queen of Sheba through their son Menelik I.) Therefore, long after its political and economic stars had faded, Axum remained a major religious center especially significant to the ongoing relationship between church and state.

I was fascinated by these foundational stories and their impact on Ethiopian Christianity. But St. Mary's is an odd place for a non-believer to "visit," especially after the accessible riches of the ruins. The chapel of the Ark—let alone the Ark itself—is off-limits to everyone except a single caretaker priest, so there is no question of seeing anything related to the relic. Nevertheless, guides and priests believe that visitors, especially Ethiopian visitors, wish to get as close to the building as they possibly can. Jean and I were thus solemnly directed to benches a few feet from the iron fence surrounding the chapel. Once seated, we were allowed to study the chapel's blank western wall in silence for a few minutes. Then, a priest in resplendent purple robes and dark sunglasses began to display treasury items like crosses and coronation crowns from the old St. Mary's (off-limits to women) on a wooden table set up just inside the fence, and our guide started in on a long and thoroughly Axumite mix of information and legend.

Did we know how the Ark had come to Ethiopia? Our guide recounted the story and cited a book on the topic by a British journalist, as though the book's foreign authorship validated the legend.

Did we know how the keeper priest was selected? The incumbent priest identified his successor, usually a young boy, who would reveal himself to the incumbent as God's choice. The boy was then put through years of training during which he was at times physically restrained lest he try to escape his demanding future.

Did we want proof of the Ark's potency? We need only consider the high incidence of blindness in Axum: the Ark was removed from the chapel once a year, during the festival of Timket, when overnight prayer vigils culminate in a dawn procession of priests carrying a church's *tabot*, its replica of the tablets inside the Ark, to a nearby lake or river where Christ's baptism is reenacted. Each year, our guide confided, lowering his voice for emphasis, one or two people in Axum were foolish enough to try to steal a glance at the passing relic. These people were instantly struck blind.

I didn't believe a word of it, of course, but I did my best to feel the significance of place. So many people believe in these stories, even today. Even if the Ark of the Covenant was not in the chapel, wasn't what mattered that people believed? Shouldn't I be able to sense, and appreciate, the holiness of a place invested with such faith? An Ethiopian couple had joined us on the bench and sat rapturously through the presentation. When the guide suggested that we conclude by purchasing vials of water blessed by St. Mary's priests, the couple practically leapt to their feet. Agnostic to faith and almost embarrassed by their enthusiasm, I followed in silence.

But I did not need to be moved by St. Mary's or believe in the stories to appreciate their significance. The Ethiopia that I know through my family, especially through my father, is the Axumite Ethiopia of expansive ancient empire and Christian kingdom. Had my father been with us in Axum, I think he would have exulted in the ruins, prayed at the churches, listened bemusedly to the stories and bought a vial of holy water. That is, he would have been completely at ease with these two sides of Axum. And because I have inherited so much of what I feel about Ethiopia from him, I too recognize the country that was born in Axum and nurtured on the plateaus of the central and northern highlands, the one that was forged in the crucible of Christianity and religious wars fought against pagan rebels and Muslim warriors. I recognize the nation that cherishes its unique history, indigenous culture and religion, and that in modern times incorporated diverse populations from the Red Sea coast to the Kenyan and Somali borders with Amharic as its lingua franca. Even if I may never be totally at ease within it, this Ethiopia does ring true to me.

But not every Ethiopian feels as I do. And the extent to which this was evident in Axum itself was the final lesson of the ancient town.

First, it is not possible to be in Axum for five minutes without thinking about Eritrea, whose separation from Ethiopia is the very antithesis of Axumite empire. At one point in our visit, we paused to take in a view of the open countryside from ruins located on a hilltop just outside town. In the distance, to the northeast, our guide pointed out the plains toward Adwa, the site of Emperor Menelik's decisive battle against the Italian army. Squinting in the midday sun, I saw arid, brown-yellow fields dotted with pale green shrubs and taller eucalyptus trees that stretched on until the plains collided with a distant mountain range. I could easily imagine the broad plain as the stage for a turn-of-the-century showdown, with Ethiopian patriots fighting to the death to preserve their independence. Less easy to imagine was the more recent Ethiopian-Eritrean clash, fought just a little further north, between soldiers whose grandfathers fought the Italians at battles across northern Ethiopia. By all accounts, the border war took thousands of lives and further impoverished two nations totally unable to afford the drain on their resources. What had inspired soldiers on both sides to defend a border that slices through the very heart of the ancient Axumite kingdom?

Eritrea's war of secession—or, depending on your point of view, its war of liberation—is an explosive topic that touches on sensitive issues of national and personal identity and pits those who accept the vision of the nation grounded in Axumite history and legend against those who do not. Now entrenched in the form of an international border, the divide between Eritrea and the rest of Ethiopia has had many consequences. It means a hardening of views, so that Eritreans and Ethiopians find it harder and harder to empathize with each other, and intermarriages and friendships have come under intense pressure. It means a ban on cross-border ownership, so that the nationals of one country who once owned homes or businesses in the other have lost lifetimes of investment. It means divided families, as restrictions on cross-border travel have forced people who come from one country but now live in the other to either forego visiting parents and childhood homes on one side of the border or give up jobs and new lives with spouses and children on the other. Finally, it means lasting sorrow to those who mourn the dismemberment of the single nation. Fourteen years after Eritrean independence, my father cannot look at a map of the Horn of Africa without wincing at the new shape of his old country, altered forever.

For Eritrean secessionists, regional experience as the basis for the national unit obviously trumped the appeal of the expansive nation born in Axum. In terms of history, Eritreans focus on the periods after the decline of Axum when the Christian kingdom did not always control the coastal regions, while their recent history is informed by the experience, unique to them, of Italian rule. Religion is also relevant. Although Eritrea has about the same percentage of Christians and Muslims as the rest of Ethiopia, Eritrea's Muslims have ties to Ethiopia's Muslim neighbors (who provided assistance to the secessionists) and a sense of pan-Islamic identity, whereas Ethiopian Oromo Muslims of the central and southern provinces practice a more localized form of Islam. Finally, there is language. The primary language of Eritrea is Tigrinya, and Eritreans have chafed at the use of Amharic, the mother tongue of about forty percent of Ethiopia's overall population, as Ethiopia's national language. In short, Eritrean secessionists did not feel a shared national history that placed them within a unified Ethiopian nation. For these Eritreans, the most significant consequence of secession is the liberation of a separate people and the lasting joy of national independence.

Always the distanced observer, I had previously regretted Eritrean independence only to the extent that I think it is a mistake for African nations to follow an ethnicist logic that focuses people on fighting each other for a greater share of national resources rather than working together to grow the common wealth. For my father and other Ethiopians for whom there is no distance between identity and country, by contrast, Eritrean secession is felt as a deep, personal loss. As I began to understand and feel the national and personal identities at stake, I began also to understand the depth of his feeling—and to realize that others might feel the opposite just as deeply.

Beyond the loss of Eritrea, historic Axumite Ethiopia is also challenged by the regionalism that pervades present-day Axum. This regionalism manifests itself most obviously through language. As in Eritrea, the primary language in Axum and the rest of Tigre province (killil) is Tigrinya, not Amharic. I did not truly appreciate this fact or its implications until the end of our first day, when, after our Amharic-speaking guide left us, we had a drink on the terrace of the Yeha hotel, which Tadesse had recommended for its lovely view of the obelisks and the churches (and also because he built it). When the last of the day's heat had melted away, we roused ourselves and walked from the Yeha to our hotel through streets revived by the cool night air. Adults visited in front of homes and shops that had been lifeless in the afternoon, and teenagers talked and laughed in loud, flirtatious exchanges. The town looked and felt much like Gondar or Bahr Dar, which we would visit in the coming days—except that everyone spoke Tigrinya. During that walk, and in later encounters in town, I suddenly found myself an outsider in a way I had not expected. I was in Ethiopia, but I didn't understand a word as people around me chatted and called to one another, and I felt as foreign as my Greek-Armenian husband.

The experience was revelatory. I felt a new empathy for Ethiopians who do not speak Amharic or speak it as a second language, and a fresh appreciation for the complaints minorities have voiced about their relationship with the language of the majority and thus with the identity of the nation. But what really threw me off was the unmistakable hostility aimed at Amharic speakers—at me. At the Axum telecommunications center, the officials who examined my passport and the employees who placed my call to Addis Ababa were curt and rude, while they were polite and friendly to others. In a convenience store, the shopowner sold a bottle of water to me, who asked for it in Amharic, for fifty percent more than he sold one to Jean, who the following day asked for one in a mixture of English and sign language. At the airport, a manager gave me a much harder time for not having observed the rule that passengers arrive two hours before departure than I suspect he would ever have given a Tigrinya speaker. Having never before personally experienced any division between Tigrinya and Amharic speakers, I was distressed to find that divide translated into concrete rebuffs. Of course these were small snubs, but they were dismaying nevertheless. And in the extent of my dismay at such insignificant slights, I could see how easily the seeds of serious linguistic and ethnic tension could take root.

My experience of modern Axum forced me to rethink my assumptions about the legitimacy and power of the region's historical and religious legacies. I left Axum wondering whether the familiar Ethiopia—the one I'd held in my head all these years—had ever been as widely recognized as I had assumed. There are many non-Amharic speakers in Ethiopia, even more non-Christians and plenty of people in regions that became a part of the country long after Axum's decline. Do these Ethiopians view their country as Axumite in origin and identity? More to the point, Tigre province, like Eritrea, for years supported a liberation front that dropped its regional demands only when its leaders seized control of Addis Ababa. Ethnic and linguistic groups in other regions have organized themselves as such to fight for rights that range from increased cultural recognition to greater regional autonomy, and even secession. I was not quite welcome in Axum, although I am a highlander who shares the same cultural history as the town's modern inhabitants, if not the same mother tongue. In the face of such fractured allegiance, can Axumite history really anchor a unified national identity? And if they cannot find it in Axum, where can the incredibly diverse people of Ethiopia find a common denominator, a shared tie, to bind them as a single nation?

* * *

On our final morning in town, Jean and I woke at dawn to hunt out one last site of ancient Axum. Our quarry was the "Lioness of Gobedra," a stone etching of a lioness, some two thousand years old.

The hotel clerk told us that the etching was a short walk west of town and assured us that we could not miss it. Forty-five minutes later, however, we had passed the Dungur palace, the outer stelae fields and even the old granite quarries, and had still not found the lioness. We had only a few hours before our plane left for Lalibela, a couple of passing trucks had covered us in huge clouds of fine dust and the temperature was already climbing. Just as we had begun to think of turning back, a little boy materialized out of the empty brown fields and sidled up to me.

The boy, who was not more than four or five years old, wore a loose blue button-down shirt, baggy shorts and clear plastic sandals, clothes that emphasized how small he was. As he edged closer, I noticed that he wore a silver cross around his neck.

We looked at each other for a moment. *"Tenastilign,"* I said gently, when it became clear that he would not be the first to speak.

The boy did not answer. Instead, he pointed up at the hillside.

I wondered what on earth this little boy was doing alone out here in the morning on a school day. I tried again. "Tell me, what is it we can do for you?"

The boy shook his head and again pointed up the hill without uttering a sound. He then took a few steps in the direction he had pointed.

"I don't think he understands me—he probably speaks Tigrinya," I said to Jean. "So I'm not sure. But I think he wants to take us to the lioness." I found something charming in the boy's silent certainty about our destination, and we agreed to follow him for fifteen minutes. When I nodded at him, he trotted off, quickly veering onto a footpath that followed a gentle ascent up the mountain face. He kept up a brisk pace as he led us through acacia trees and around residential yards attended by squawking chickens and the occasional dog, looking back every few minutes to make sure we were still there. He seemed quite sure of himself, but fifteen minutes later there was still no sign of the lioness.

"I hope this little kid isn't taking us to some big brother and his friends—now that would be a great careless-tourist story," Jean muttered.

I considered this possibility—I had felt uneasy in Ethiopia, not least of all in Axum, but not once had I felt unsafe. But perhaps the boy and I had misunderstood each other.

Just then, above us on the hill, we saw an elderly man driving a pair of gaunt cows down the path. The old man was thin, as wiry as his cattle, with matchstick legs visible beneath a pair of short cotton pants. Wisps of gray hair had escaped from under the turban he wore despite the heat, and he leaned on a heavy stick as he walked.

"Good—you can ask this man for help," said Jean.

"What if he doesn't speak Amharic?" My protest was immediate.

"Well, you'll find out. Rebecca, he won't hurt you."

I truly was reluctant to speak Amharic to another stranger after my experiences in town. I just did not want to be rebuffed over language again. But neither did I want to turn back, as we would have had to do if we missed this chance for help. So I stepped ahead on the path, in front of the little boy.

"*Tenastilign*, my father, how are you," I began, speaking slowly and as politely as I knew how. "*Yikirta yadrgulign*—please, do forgive me. I do not speak Tigrinya. I only speak Amharic."

I paused for a reaction, but the old man just held my gaze and waited. Suddenly I felt quite conscious of the dust that covered my face, my hair, my white t-shirt.

"We are searching for the lion, the one made of stone," I continued. "They tell us that it is here in the mountains. Could you tell us—is it right, our path?"

The old man's response was the complete opposite of everything I had feared. He transferred his walking stick to his left hand, straightened his stooped shoulders and gravely extended a rough, calloused hand. Only after he had released my hand from this formal greeting did he speak, confirming in careful, halting Amharic that we were in fact on the right path. I thanked him profusely, we wished each other well, and he was gone.

And indeed, a few minutes later, in an otherwise unremarkable spot amidst the mountain shrubs, our little guide triumphantly marched up to the lioness. She was etched into a large, bell-shaped slab of gray stone mottled with veins of blue and green that glinted in the morning sun, depicted in a full, muscular run so that her body extended about three meters from her open jaws to her trailing tail. Someone had carved a crusader's cross a few inches above and to the right of her head, but otherwise her solitude was complete. No one knows who is responsible for this lovely, lonely piece of art—the lioness could be a pagan idol, the symbol of a powerful king, or perhaps the personal creation of a talented mason. Beautiful and enigmatic, high in her spot above the Gondar road, she remains a particularly intriguing piece of the Axumite puzzle.

I was delighted that we had found the etching, enchanted with the little boy who did not need language to communicate, and touched by the old shepherd whose rough hand softened the distress I'd felt in the town. It had been a full and complicated visit, and I was content to carry away the lioness, the boy and the old man as my parting images of historic Axum.

With my father, 1965.

With my grandmother and two cousins, 1966.

With my mother, 1967.

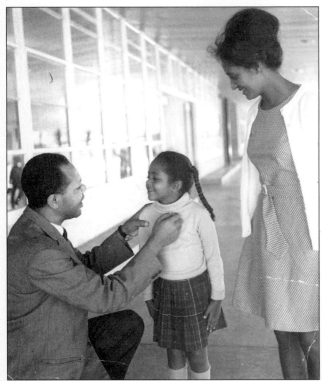

With my parents on the first day of school, 1970.

The house my parents built.

With Jean in the garden of our house.

My grandmother.

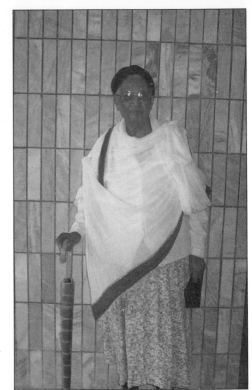

Cutting the cake at my
grandmother's house.

Tye Ityobia.

Tadesse in his office.

"King Ezana's" obelisk, Axum.

Jean with the young guide who led us to the lioness, outside Axum.

Bete Giyorgis
church, Lalibela.

Monk at prayer,
Lalibela. The niche
behind holds human
remains.

A stop on Tadesse's road, outside Lalibela.

Tadesse's bridge, near Lalibela airport.

Bete Maryam, Zege peninsula, Lake Tana.

Disembarking at Kibran Gabriel, Lake Tana.

Narga Selassie church, Lake Tana.

Dek Island (Narga Selassie) dock, Lake Tana.

The Moon over Lake Tana

We had been motoring north for about half an hour when Yohannes, our boatsman, pointed out an object in the distance. It was a *tankwa*, the distinctive papyrus reed vessel that villagers have used on the lake for centuries. As we drew closer, Jean and I made out a delicate hybrid, a cross between a canoe and a raft. It had low-slung sides that were nearly level with the water and a pointed bow that rose a foot or so above. At each end, on either side of a precarious-looking stack of firewood, sat a man with a kayak-style oar. Yohannes told us that the men were traveling from villages along the distant shores of the lake to the town of Bahr Dar, in the south, where they would sell the firewood for a few *birr* and perhaps shop for goods to transport home. The villagers do not have many other sources of income and so men like these undertook the laborious trip across the lake once or twice each week. We spotted several *tankwas* that morning, each one quiet confirmation that we had indeed arrived in a place only lightly touched by time.

We were on Lake Tana, a vast, heart-shaped body of water located in northwest Ethiopia. Outside Ethiopia, the lake is known as the source of the Blue Nile, the mighty river which tumbles south and west from the lake until it meets up with the White Nile several thousand kilometers later. Within Ethiopia, the region is also known as an important center of Ethiopian Christianity, a place where monks, monarchs and ordinary men have come to seek sanctuary from the secular world. Tradition holds that even the Ark of the Covenant was once protected by the lake—concealed, the monks say, inside the remote island monastery of Tana Cherqos for nearly five hundred years.

Ethiopian Orthodox Christianity and the Church are fundamental elements of Ethiopian history and culture. Ethiopia's nation-defining struggles, prior to the appearance of the colonial powers, were wars of religion, like the bloody sixteenth-century wars with the rebel armies of the Muslim leader Ahmed ibn Ibrahim—or Ahmed Gragn, Ahmed the Left-Handed, as he is known in the Ethiopian chronicles. Ethiopian kings and queens, virtually all of whom were Orthodox, claimed a divine right to the throne through the Axumite legends linking the royal line to King Solomon of Jerusalem. With the exception of the monuments and ruins of Axum's pre-Christian civilization, nearly all of Ethiopia's important historic sites are Christian. Ethiopian literature and art are almost exclusively religious works; only in modern times have artists addressed secular subjects. Over one half of all Ethiopians are Orthodox Christians, and the percentage is higher in the central and northern highlands. In Amharic, you can't greet someone—*tenastilign*, literally "May He give you health on my behalf"—or thank her—*ighzeryistilign*, literally "May God reward you on my behalf"—without invoking God.

Faith and the Church are just as important to my family. For most, Christianity is an essential, a given. My parents' characters, and the decisions they have made over the years, are so informed by faith that I can't imagine who they would be without this central touchstone. For my father, the Church as an institution has also been crucial. The Church helped him exchange rural poverty for doctoral degrees and a university professorship. He fell in love with the Church's Ge'ez language and liturgy and dedicated his life to the study of its texts and traditions. He grew very close to the Abuna, the head of the Church, becoming his confidante and unofficial lay representative. It is ironic that ties to such a fundamentally Ethiopian institution should lead to his exile, but those ties are almost certainly why he became a Derg target. During his short service in the post-revolutionary National Parliament, he protested certain anti-Church proposals, such as a proposed Derg veto over the appointment of bishops; that opposition undoubtedly angered Mengistu and led to my father's arrest. But when he began looking for work outside Ethiopia, the international religious network he had established through years of representing the Church abroad quite literally achieved his salvation by finding him a new home within the Catholic community of Minnesota's St. John's University.

Nothing of this sort is true of me. Certainly, I grew up aware of faith as a basic part of everyday life—we celebrated religious holidays and observed fasts, started meals with prayers of thanks my father made us memorize and invoked God's name in ordinary conversation. My father occasionally took me along on his visits to the Abuna and I can still recall the resplendent ceremonial chamber where the patriarch received us, clad in his austere black robes and high black turban. But my sister and I did not get much exposure to the actual Church or get properly initiated in its rituals. My parents did not take us to regular services, which last about three hours, knowing that we would fidget through them, and the Church did not have a tradition of classes for children. In fact, I can remember attending a proper church service just twice—first for the baptism of my infant sister, a pre-dawn service in a dark basement chapel filled with clouds of acrid incense, and then for Mimi and Tadesse's wedding, a glorious midday service during which I stood for what felt like forever in a long line of bridesmaids. I'm not sure whether or how my parents intended to provide us with religious instruction as we grew older, but in any event by 1975 the Derg had put an end to any such plans.

As I grew older, the Church felt increasingly distant. In the United States we had few chances to attend Ethiopian Orthodox services. My brother, who was born in America, was not baptized until he was four years old, when my parents obtained permission from St. John's for a visiting Armenian Orthodox bishop to perform the ceremony in the Catholic baptistery. Distance from the Church and ignorance of its rituals became a large part of the cultural distancing I came to feel when I was around other Ethiopians. Moreover, as I developed the perspective of a Western-educated woman, I grew wary of the Church as a political and social institution. The Church has rarely used its power and prestige to tackle, for example, the problems of poverty, illiteracy and poor health that plague Ethiopia. I even came to think that the Church was an antiquated religious institution, quite out of touch with the evolving needs of its constituents. In making this point, I often described my dismay at the wedding of a cousin and her American fiancé several years earlier.

The Ethiopian Orthodox priest who officiated began with a full mass in Ge'ez, and then gave his homily in Amharic. That is, he chose to stick with the traditional marriage ceremony even though half the people in the church—including the poor groom—did not speak Amharic and no one in the pews understood a word of Ge'ez, a language that is written, not spoken. When the priest finally switched to English, he offered a short sermon about the blessed nature of marriage, in which he defined a woman's role as following her husband's lead at all times. I left the ceremony upset, ever a stranger to the Church's rituals and even more skeptical of the framework the Church offers its followers.

So I wasn't thinking about the Church when I planned my trip to Ethiopia. But from the moment we landed in Addis Ababa, I felt the Church at every turn. Driving home from the airport that first Sunday, I saw the breadth of the Church's appeal in the crowds leaving churches after morning services. In my aunt's house, I saw the depth of the devotion it could inspire in the dressing alcove Mimi had converted into an intimate, oft-visited shrine to the Virgin Mary. Nearly everyone I met was a believer, and the churches of Addis Ababa were thronged with worshippers no matter what day or time we visited. For some, like my grandmother, Church and faith are constants that have never wavered or changed, no matter the political or economic crises of the day; for others, like my aunt, faith has taken on a greater role, perhaps to counter the displacement and trauma of the revolution. Very quickly, I was reminded just how tightly the Ethiopia I know is intertwined with the Church I'd set aside. By the time we were buying airplane tickets to Bahr Dar and the other cities of the north, I understood that my trip would not be the secular pilgrimage I had imagined. If I meant to experience Ethiopia I would have to experience the Church, and nowhere is that truer than on Lake Tana.

Ethiopian history and culture are reflected in the churches and monasteries that cover the country, and the churches of

Lake Tana are no exception. Beyond that, however, the island churches have a special allure rooted in their physical setting. The protective waters of the lake have kept these churches isolated and unchanged for centuries; they are tended today by priests and monks who look, live and worship as have generations of clergy before them. These churches thus suggested the timelessness of the larger Church, a timelessness which in turn seemed to promise us a glimpse of the institution at its most fundamental. Moreover, my experience of these churches was uniquely framed by the long, slow journey required to reach them. Once on the lake, Jean and I became passive passengers with nothing but the waves to watch and our destination to think about. The secular world and its everyday distractions were gone; only the silent *tankwas*, those delicate vessels from an earlier time, crossed this fluid filter. After the work involved in traveling first to Ethiopia and then to Bahr Dar, in booking flights and finding hotels and negotiating fares, boating across Lake Tana calmed us so that we arrived at the islands still of soul and open to every possibility.

The gateway to the lake is the modern town of Bahr Dar, literally, "sea's edge." Even on a Sunday afternoon, the town was lively. Its many churches, outdoor markets, hotels and restaurants and its wide palm-tree-lined avenues were full of people enjoying the fine dry-season weather. We took a room at the Ghion Hotel, a popular waterfront motel with landscaped gardens and a cheerful outdoor café. Scruffy European backpackers in shorts and sandals wandered the grounds, while a dozen or so older men and women in crisp khakis and modest skirts, most likely missionaries, or perhaps employees of a local NGO, chatted over afternoon tea. Down at the Ghion's dock, young Ethiopian men stripped off their Sunday clothes to jump in the lake, splashing and shouting, while groups of women watched discreetly from under shade trees at the water's edge. A hotel radio broadcast international music and programs (including, strangely, from a Turkish station), giving the whole place the feel of an on-going summer party.

The Ghion's owners introduced us to Yohannes, a handsome man in his early twenties, and together we planned a full day's itinerary on the lake. We decided on Bete Giyorgis, Bete Maryam and Ura Kidane Mihret, three churches clustered together on nearby Zege peninsula; the church and monastery of Narga Selassie, located on an islet next to the large island of Dek near the middle of the lake, and the secluded monastery of Kibran Gabriel, on a tiny island just thirty minutes from Bahr Dar.

We met at the hotel dock early the next morning. Yohannes loaded lifejackets and extra jerrycans of gasoline into his blue and white *jelba*, a picturesque wooden motorboat with unpadded benches and a white canvas tarp stretched over a metal frame, while we got the hotel to pack us a picnic lunch. Once underway, I quickly came under the spell of the lake. First Bahr Dar disappeared, and then the lakeshore to the east and west faded from view. Soon, as the sun climbed overhead, all we could see in any direction was pale slate-blue water against an even paler sky. Save for the occasional brown pelican floating lazily overhead, and the *tankwas* gliding noiselessly past, we were the only ones on the water. As we motored on, I imagined that we were leaving behind our everyday selves. I closed my eyes to the equatorial sun on my face and trailed my fingers in the cool clear water, savoring the anticipation of what was to come.

This sense of possibility remained until we neared the Zege dock.

"Look at all those people," Jean said, sitting up and pointing to the pier. "They aren't waiting for us, are they?" About twenty-five people, mostly young adults and children, were standing on or just beyond the dock. As we came closer, seven or eight young men began jostling each other for position and shouting to us.

"Here! Here! Yohannes—throw me your rope! Let me tie it for you!"

"Let me guard the boat!"

"Let me be your guide! I will take you to the church!"

Yohannes cut the motor and pulled in behind the several boats already docked at the pier. When I stood up, half a dozen hands reached out to help me climb out of the *jelba*.

"*Simu*! Listen!" I said, trying to sound as definitive as I could. "We really don't need a guide. And we're not going to buy anything—not one thing."

The boys ignored me and stayed in step around us as we walked down the pier and onto the grassy clearing between the water and the woods. One young man walked right in front of me, loudly instructing us to watch our step here and avoid that branch there; I heard another whisper to Yohannes to intervene with us on his behalf. Younger children tugged at our shirts to show us the little silver crosses and rings they had for sale. My spirits sank—there was nothing beautiful in this introduction to Zege, much less spiritual or sacred.

"Tell them a big boat with twenty Americans is just ten minutes behind us," advised Jean, who didn't seem bothered by the attention. "If they follow us to the churches, they're going to miss the real spenders." As for Yohannes, I thought I felt his divided loyalties. Alone in the boat, we'd shared friendly conversation and our picnic lunch (he had accepted a sandwich, and also a banana, throwing the peel over the side of the boat and laughing out loud when I reflexively muttered something Western and ridiculous about our shared responsibility to keep the lake clean. "The fish will eat it," he said, smiling.). He did not like to see us harassed, but he could not side with us over people he knew, especially since we were obviously paying him for his services. He remained silent, eyes cast down.

The churches were clustered in clearings near the top of a hill about twenty-five minutes up a path that cut through deep green coffee plants and fragrant mango, lemon and orange trees. The Lake Tana region is one of the few places where Ethiopia's original tree cover still survives and the fruit trees were a welcome respite from the blue leaves and medicinal scent of the ubiquitous eucalyptus. The children followed us all the way to the compound gates where a stern deacon finally waved them off. The deacon exchanged our admission *birr* for carefully stamped receipts and admitted us into the compound. A second priest waiting beside the church door asked us to take off our shoes—invisible angels are said to attend Ethiopian churches, and the faithful remove their shoes so as not to harm them—and then extended his cross to Yohannes and me. At the entrance to each of the three churches, Yohannes lowered his head so that a priest could touch a cross to his forehead and lips in the customary ritual. And each time, not knowing how else to decline the blessing and not even certain which part of my face the cross was supposed to touch first, I stepped awkwardly aside.

Free of the crowds and past the priests and deacons, we were finally able to explore the churches of Zege. The three churches probably date from the late sixteenth and early seventeenth centuries, a period when the Christian kingdom was slowly recovering from the devastation unleashed by Ahmed

109

Gragn, and all three are fine examples of Lake Tana architecture and art. The churches are perfect circles, small and beautifully proportioned, with conical thatched roofs of rough brown straw. Their interiors are divided into three concentric areas: an outer circle, where worshippers stand during services and cantors sing hymns; an inner circle, where priests prepare and administer communion, and finally the *meqdes*, the innermost sanctuary where the *tabot*, a slab of engraved wood or stone, is stored inside a wooden cupboard. As it does for other early Christian churches, the *tabot* serves as an altar stone for priests to use during the Eucharistic liturgy. However, unique to the Ethiopian Orthodox Church, the *tabot* is also considered a church's replica of the Tables of Law contained inside the original Ark of the Covenant. It is the object that invests each church with holiness—a church without a *tabot* cannot be a place of worship.

The church interiors were covered with carvings and painted murals, most probably dating from the eighteenth and nineteenth centuries. The carvings framed the door and windows in knotted, repetitive geometric motifs that were picked up in the shape of small exterior windows through which narrow shafts of light penetrated the dim interiors. The murals, some painted directly onto the church walls and others onto billowing squares of fabric suspended from wooden poles, were distinctly Ethiopian. The most recognizable elements were the flat frontal figures with narrow faces, dark, defined almond eyes and long, tapering fingers. The colors were vivid, saturated shades of yellow, red, green and blue, with heavy black lines used to outline shapes and demarcate different panels. Outer panels were covered with the geometric motifs, while central panels depicted stories from the Gospels or scenes from the lives of Ethiopian saints, like St. George, shown on his white horse, slaying the dragon, or St. Gebre Menfes Qiddus, shown always among lions, leopards and other wild beasts. Another favorite subject was the life of the Virgin Mary, whom Orthodox Ethiopians venerate, shown alone or with her son, working miracles or interceding on behalf of the pleading faithful. In all, the interiors contained intense bursts of artistic expression inspired by the celebration of religion.

After we had toured the churches, the deacon took us to a separate building where crosses, manuscripts, chalices, crowns and other objects from each church's treasury had been laid out. I found the manuscripts especially fascinating. My father has spent years studying microfilmed versions of such books at an institute affiliated with St. John's University in Minnesota, of all unlikely places, and it was thrilling to see the heavy wooden books, with their frayed parchment pages and thick leather straps, in their intended setting. I also liked the intricately carved silver and gold crowns—one particularly memorable headpiece was shaped like an onion dome and topped with a detailed, matchbox-size replica of the Ark. The priests did not attribute the crowns to any specific king or queen, but several famous monarchs are buried in lake monasteries: Yekunno Amlak, who overthrew the Zagwes and "reestablished" the Solomonic/Axumite dynasty; Za'ra Ya'kob, under whose leadership Church scholars and scribes produced unprecedented numbers of religious books, and Fasiledes, who from his medieval palace in nearby Gondar provided generous support to the lake's monastic communities.

Every aspect of the three churches—their traditional architecture, their paintings, the contents of their treasuries, their association with kings and queens and saints, the rich legends and literature they have supported—underscored the nexus between the Church and Ethiopia. I felt proud of this indigenous Ethiopian culture and history; on this score I felt no ambivalence toward the Church. Moreover, standing between piercing shafts of sunshine in the dim outer circles, studying the stories of faith depicted in the exuberant murals, contemplating the sacred *meqdes* and the claimed link between this ancient Church and the Temple of Jerusalem, I could feel the powerful allure of that culture.

Over the centuries, isolated from other Christian centers, the Ethiopian state and the Ethiopian Church fought parallel battles of survival. The Church's traditions are thus nearly inseparable from Ethiopian traditions, and in a flash I saw how my criticism of the Church as out of touch with its modern congregants might be quite beside the point: the Church is as much about culture and national and individual identity as it is about religion and faith. In times of upheaval, of which Ethiopia has seen more than its share, those traditions and that identity, rooted as they are in a realm beyond the world of absolute monarchs and brutal militaries, must be particularly seductive.

What I didn't get from Zege, however, was a feeling of spirituality. To the contrary, the peninsula churches seemed in danger of having their beauty and allure overwhelmed by pedestrian commercialism. The aggressive crowds colored my entire experience; the efficient deacons and priests at the churches made it abundantly clear that we should tip them; we could not even get inside the churches without paying an admission fee.

"Why does it bother you so much?" Jean pressed me when I kept grumbling about the crowds. "Anywhere you go, there's always someone trying to make money from a holy site. Plus, we *are* tourists. You, too—you don't even know how to kiss the cross. Why should it be different here?"

Why? Because even if I don't like having a cross pushed on me, I am Ethiopian, and I was "home," in my country and among my Church's monuments. I suppose I had hoped for the freedom that "home" implies, and something about the restful water crossing had permitted me to believe that this was possible. I had wanted to walk undisturbed through the lemon trees and coffee plants as my believer parents might have done, to try to feel what they might have felt—maybe even to take away a little of what they might have taken.

Back in Addis Ababa, we'd gone to visit St. Giyorgis church one afternoon. As we approached the church, Mimi had made Jean lie down in the backseat of her car until she had driven past the group of almseekers near the gate. She did this not to avoid giving money—in Ethiopia it is customary to give before entering a church, and everyone, especially Mimi, carries coins for this purpose—but to avoid the frenzy that foreigners always trigger. At Zege, Jean and I were both foreigners, and my experience of the peninsula churches was framed by the frenzy that greeted us.

Our next stop was Narga Selassie church. Narga Selassie is located on an islet near Dek Island, a beautiful green island near the very center of the lake. Unlike the Zege peninsula, remote Dek has only one church, a tiny permanent population and very few visitors. The island seemed to me to be in much greater harmony than the Zege peninsula with the sensibility fostered by the open waters of the lake, and my experience of its church was dramatically different.

As we pulled up to the island's stone pier, several men who had been watching our approach helped Yohannes secure the boat. This time there was no jostling or shouting, just polite assistance. Once we had disembarked, a monk wearing a turban, a cotton shawl and short pants that revealed knobby knees, greeted us and shyly invited us to follow him through an attractive stone arch we had noticed from the lake. The arch resembled a medieval bell tower or sentry post, and it made a lovely entry to the wooded island. The church was located just beyond, inside a shaded stone compound. Save for the men who had met our boat, and who trailed discreetly behind us, we were alone. The place was peaceful and picturesque, and it felt wonderful to stroll under the shade trees after sitting for so long in the boat.

After a few minutes of wandering around, I noticed the monk whispering urgently to Yohannes on the other side of the compound. Yohannes appeared animated in his response, gesticulating at the monk and the other men in the group until one of them trotted off.

"The monk says the church is locked," Yohannes said, as I crossed over to the group. "They're trying to find the priest with the key."

As a rule, Ethiopian churches are kept locked unless a service is underway, and only one or two priests are allowed a copy of the key. The Church adopted this policy a few years back to combat the theft of religious artifacts—a huge problem, given the combination of local poverty and lucrative international markets. I had just read a long article my father had written about the serious cultural and historical loss associated with the disappearance of manuscripts.

"I've told them before that someone with the key should always stay close." Yohannes muttered this as much to himself as to me.

"He will be here soon, my sister, in just a minute or two," said the monk anxiously, his eyes going from Yohannes' face to mine. "Please, come, let us show you and your—your husband—the compound."

We let the monk point out the exterior features of the church—he was especially proud to describe a project underway to replace the ugly corrugated tin roof with yellow straw, the original roofing material. Then we agreed to go look at items in the church's treasury, which the priests were storing in a separate building during the roof restoration. It was a pretty walk—we took a shaded footpath, flanked by fruit trees and tall native grasses, across a miniature archipelago of islands connected by swaying wooden footbridges. As we walked, one of the men in our group shouted out the keeper priest's name at the top of his lungs, again and again: "Abba! Abba!" Occasionally, we heard responses that bounced back at us across land and water. The shouting prompted Yohannes to say to me wryly, "You see, Ribka? We too have our cellular telephones."

At the treasury building, the poor monk did all he could to buy time for the keeper priest to be found. He drew out his presentation, but eventually we had seen every single item and examined every single illuminated manuscript page. Desperate, the monk then dug through the folds of his shawl and produced three fat lemons.

"Would you like some lemons?" he asked hopefully.

"Lemons?"

"Yes. These lemons grow here, here on the blessed island of Narga Selassie," he said. "These lemons are holy lemons."

"Uh—*ishe*. All right. *Igzeryistilign*," I said. The monk beamed as I took two lemons and dropped them into my bag.

"Father! Please!" Yohannes interjected. "Leave alone the lemons, and just find the key!" He was clearly worried about our reaction if, after paying for and making the long trip, we did not get inside the church.

The crestfallen monk tucked away the last lemon and marched us slowly back to the main church. After a bit more standing around and a few more delay tactics, Jean and I decided we had to go. We got back in our boat and had motored a few meters into the lake when the men who had been waving from the dock began shouting: "Return, return! The priest has been found!" And so, having come so far to see Narga Selassie church, we turned back.

I was glad we did. Like the churches of Zege, Narga Selassie is round, built atop a stepped foundation made of the same yellow stone. From the outside, the church is petite and alluring, in perfect harmony with its wooded setting. On the inside, it is extensively decorated with carved wood and vivid paintings, two of which I especially liked. The first was of the Egyptian army chasing the Israelites across the Red Sea in the moment just after the parted waters of the sea rushed back together again. The artist had conveyed the Egyptians' defeat by painting tens of colorful helmeted heads and the tips of muskets and bayonets bobbing along the swollen blue sea, detached from the bodies below, creating an effect that was both powerful and playful. The second was of a strange character, a fat toad of a man seated cross-legged, naked save for a bright red sash draped across his chest and waist, shown holding his huge protruding tongue in one hand and a long, curved knife in the other. According to the deacon, this man was a sinner punished for consuming the flesh of humans. As with the Red Sea painting, I liked the contrast between the serene church and the savage image. In both cases the artists had shown the messy side of religion, the domain of sinners, of conflict and of grotesque moments—much more interesting, I thought, than another painting of a benevolent Virgin.

In all, I fell a little bit in love with Narga Selassie. Like the
Zege churches, the church testified to the Church's accomplishments, but unlike those churches, Narga Selassie felt to
me like a true retreat, a place where spirituality was at the fore.
No crowds distracted us, no priests mediated our visit. And
the earnest, anxious monk, with his short pants and fumbling
for keys and holy lemons, was an unexpected, refreshing face.
He was nothing like the efficient Zege deacons or the stern,
unapproachable priests I'd always associated with church rituals. The Church makes me so uncomfortable, makes me feel
so like an outsider, yet here was a priest who seemed to be
even less at ease than I was. The setting allowed me to explore
and experience Narga Selassie at my own pace, and I felt a
degree of affection for the Church I'd never felt before.

Narga's problems, sadly, were rooted in the very factors
that made it so attractive. The remoteness of Dek Island
allowed us a tranquil, unspoilt visit, but it means isolation
and hardship for the church and the island's residents. During our three hours there, no other boat arrived or launched.
Except for the keeper priest and one lone child, we saw no one
who hadn't been standing at the pier when we first arrived.
The desolation made the church seem more museum than
active religious center, and the island more nature preserve
than thriving village. As Yohannes pulled the boat away from
the pier for the second time, the men we'd met stayed by the
water, waving halfheartedly, until we could no longer make
them out. They quite obviously had nothing else to do and
nowhere else to go. For a moment, I almost missed the boisterous Zege kids.

Our last stop was the monastery of Kibran Gabriel, on an
islet about forty-five minutes north of Bahr Dar. By now the
sun hung low in the sky, sending rich, mellow rays across the

darkening water. The water and warm afternoon light again heightened my anticipation of what we would discover, and once again I was not disappointed. The tiny islet was even more appealing than Narga Selassie, lightly wooded with indigenous flora and the added elegance of willows and other low-branched trees that sheltered the patch of beach where we docked. The landing area was deserted, and for the first time that day we secured the boat ourselves.

Kibran Gabriel does not admit women—at one time women were not even allowed on the island. Yohannes led us up a short, steep path through the woods, then stopped at a point that wasn't marked in any way I could discern.

"Ribka, I'm sorry—you can't go any further," he said.

"I know. It's okay." This was, at that moment at least, the truth. The patriarchy of the Church and the unequal treatment of women were neither news to me nor specific to the Orthodox Church. And I had been warned about Kibran Gabriel—a monastery, after all—when we planned our tour the previous day. Moreover, a part of me was actually relieved that I didn't have to examine another church or speak to another group of priests. By the time we arrived at Kibran Gabriel, I was completely taken with the natural beauty of the lake and islands. I realized that I was responding as much to the physical surroundings as I was to the churches, perhaps because the churches and the priests required so much more from me. In any event, I welcomed the chance to sit alone and absorb more of the serene setting.

I walked back down the hill and wandered away from the shaded beach until I found a large rock on a promontory jutting out into the water, facing west. As if determined to put one last exclamation point on Lake Tana's beauty, nature put on a glorious show that seemed staged for me alone. Seated on the rock, I watched an immense red sun disappear under the lake's distant rim, the broad strokes of pinks and purples splashed across the sky reflected in broken shards of color across the water's surface, while pelicans swooped gracefully by, busy with their end-of-day feeding. A wave of gratitude washed over me. I felt privileged to have come home to Ethiopia and to Lake Tana, to have visited such beautiful churches, and to have the day end with this spectacular display. Under my breath, addressing no one in particular, I murmured my thanks for my good fortune.

A monk wrapped in a graying shawl had been watching me for some time. We had noticed him when we landed, though he hadn't approached us then. Now, a few minutes after the sun had set, he walked slowly down the promontory.

"*Tenastilign*, my sister," he said, when he was just a few feet away.

"*Tenastilign*," I answered. I rose to my feet and waited for more, but he didn't say anything. "So, you are a monk here, living on this island?" I said, after a few seconds.

"Yes," he said. "I've lived here many years, I don't remember how many."

"Where are you from?"

"Bahr Dar."

"That is where you were born?"

"Yes, I was born in a village near Bahr Dar."

"I was born in Addis Ababa," I said. He hadn't asked me the question, but I felt that it was my turn to reveal something.

"I've never been to Addis Ababa," he said. "I stay here most of the time now."

"I came here, to Lake Tana, from America," I said. "I live there now. That's where I grew up." Even with a monk

I'd never see again, I felt the need to explain my accented Amharic.

The monk looked at me blankly, as if coming from America were a possibility too far outside the world of his existence to digest, as I suppose his world was outside mine. Abruptly, he changed the subject.

"Are you Christian?" he demanded. He meant, of course, was I Ethiopian Orthodox. His direct question took me aback, but I answered it.

"Yes, I am," I said. "That's how I was raised."

"You are not Protestant?"

"No, I am not."

He studied me for a moment. He must not have believed me—perhaps my jeans and accented Amharic were incompatible with his idea of an Orthodox woman—because he continued, "You know, if you are a Protestant you should not be shy to say so. Because you wouldn't be the only one. I myself know many Ethiopians who have strayed, who have made the mistake of becoming Pente." By "Pente" I knew he meant all Protestants.

"No, I am Orthodox, I am not a Pente," I repeated, and after that there didn't seem to be much to say. I couldn't imagine getting into a discussion about my ambivalence toward the Church with him—he seemed like a person who felt his allegiances quite clearly.

Soon, Jean came back down the hill, full of enthusiasm for the monastery at the top. Kibran Gabriel is even today a thriving theological center, with a large library and approximately fifty monks in residence. Jean described an engaged and articulate English-speaking monk who had been eager to debate with him whether the Biblical statement that Jerusalem is "amidst" the world meant that the holy city is actually in the "middle" or physical "center" of the world, rather than "among" the other cities of the world, as Jean had suggested. The monk had taken Jean through a library full of illuminated manuscripts, including a manuscript with pages as big as the tanned sheep hides from which several pages are usually cut. Later, when we developed our film, I saw that Jean had photographed a manuscript in which the scribe had copied out the Bahra Hassab, the complicated Ethiopian calendar and subject of the book my father had sent to Tadesse and Mimi.

"You will be happy to know," Jean also reported, "that after all the time they spent showing me around, no one asked me for money."

"But you gave some, right?" I asked. Mimi had made us promise to make a little donation to every church we visited.

"Yes. But when I offered it to him he wouldn't take it. He showed me a box near the door and I put it in there."

It was comforting to end the day with Kibran Gabriel, a place with neither the commercialism of Zege nor the desolation of Narga Selassie. The sort of questions Kibran Gabriel raised were different, and perhaps not unique to the Ethiopian Orthodox Church. For example, how was the theological study of the monks on the island relevant outside the monastery walls? Jerusalem can be located on any map; for most people I know, the city is at the "center" of the world only in the sense that every geographical point is at the center of a globe. The monk on the beach had dedicated his life to his Church, so maybe his conviction that only the misguided could prefer Protestantism to the Church was understandable. But Protestant and Catholic missionaries have targeted Ethiopia for centuries and those churches *are* gaining ground. (Indeed, in the 1500s, Portuguese and Spanish Jesuits actually persuaded Emperor Susenyos to embrace Catholicism, although the resulting outcry forced Susenyos to abdicate in favor of his son Fasiledes, a strong supporter of the Ethiopian Orthodox Church.) My own fiercely Orthodox family now includes several fervent Protestants, all of whom can rattle off a dozen problems with the Church with the unshakable certainty of converts. Still others—like me—find the Church less and less relevant, even though they are not affirmatively attracted to other religions. The age-old traditions wrapped up in Ethiopian history are undeniably powerful, but if the Church does not reexamine its relationship with its congregants, I fear it risks further defections.

The Zege churches, Narga Selassie, Kibran Gabriel—in each case, at each stop, I felt the pull of the Church's history and culture. My chest tightened with pride at the beauty of each church and painting and cross and crown, and I left each sacred site wanting to proclaim to the world Ethiopia's accomplishments. I could see how this legacy had captured my father's heart, and how it had helped create the foundation of my parents' religious conviction. I claimed these cultural contributions as a part of my own national and personal history.

And yet, at the end of the long day on the lake, I'd also come home to a basic truth: none of what I'd seen could ever be completely mine. As a daughter of my parents and of the country, I defend my right to walk undisturbed through the Zege woods, whether I walk in search of greater understanding of nation or family or in search of spiritual clarity or personal peace. But I have not been raised in this Church and I have not taken the leap that faith requires. My admiration for the Church's cultural contributions is tempered by my despair over the Church's anachronisms and leadership in modern times. I have far too many questions and far too many doubts ever to come home to this Church. I am left to envy my parents and others for the world-ordering framework that Orthodox Christianity provides them, even as I chafe at that framework's limitations. For me, the Church is indeed a part of Ethiopia—familiar and fundamental, but not entirely mine.

* * *

During the short ride from Kibran Gabriel back to the hotel dock, the sky began to darken over the lake. Stars appeared one after the other on the deep blue stage, faint at first and then brighter, opening acts for the flat white moon that soon suspended itself before us. We motored along in silence, the only boat out on the lake, all three of us lost in private reverie. Land and the lights of Bahr Dar were well in sight when Yohannes broke the quiet.

"Ribka," he said, pointing up to the blue-black sky, "Do you believe that men have traveled to the moon?"

"Of course they have," I answered, surprised at the question. I told him that astronauts had traveled into space many times, even throwing in a description—as best I could in Amharic—of the research station (the "*bet*") the United States had left permanently up in space. But Yohannes was not persuaded.

"I do not believe that they have done it," he countered. "No. I only believe what I can see with my own eyes or what I can touch with my hands, and I can't see how it is possible to travel as far as the moon." With that, he relaxed back into the rudder with the demeanor of a man who knows he has good common sense on his side.

The seven or eight hours we had just spent together had been all about churches and monasteries and the enduring nature of religious traditions and the promise of faith. So I, in turn, asked him about God, whom he had not seen or touched but in whom he had nevertheless placed his faith. How did God differ from a trip to the moon?

Yohannes may have paused, but if he did it was only for a second. "Ah, but faith," he shrugged, "faith is different."

Lalibela and the Road Beyond

We flew to Lalibela in the late morning of a clear, sweltering day. When the pilot directed his crew to prepare for landing, we scanned the ground for the town but saw nothing, just the jagged Lasta peaks we had been flying over for the last hour. Not even a rough road was visible from the sky. The pilot gave no further warning before he banked the plane sharply and began a steep descent into a valley that suddenly split the mountain range open. A minute or two later, the plane nosed down a lone airstrip and taxied to within fifty meters of a neat concrete building that bore the sign "Lalibela." Two men dragged a stairway to the plane and within moments we were on the tarmac.

Lalibela is known for its rock monoliths, eleven massive churches carved out of giant blocks of red volcanic tufa by order of the Zagwe kings who ruled Ethiopia from the isolated mountain town from the ninth to the thirteenth century. The monoliths are Ethiopia's most famous monuments, and I could hardly believe that I would finally visit the churches I'd heard so much about. Even better, this was to be a two-part stop. My uncle's construction company was building a road in the area and he had workers and equipment stationed at a camp about 100 kilometers away. Tadesse had arranged for a car and driver to take us around Lalibela and then on to the camp so that we could tour his road and a part of rural Ethiopia not normally seen by tourists.

Two days later, I left Lalibela with beautiful and unforgettable images of both the churches and the road emblazoned in my memory. With these images, however, came equally memorable images of poverty and desolation. Lalibela is a showcase of extremes, a place where the ambitious works of devout kings and secular engineers coexist with the worst problems of a poor country. The contrast forced me to think hard about the meaning of these grand works. Could they be enjoyed for the impressive accomplishments they were, or should they be regretted as folly, given the region's urgent, unmet needs? Was Tadesse crazy to have spent a full seven years forging a road through these rough mountains, or should I applaud his perseverance?

The contrasts of the region were visible from the moment we landed. The government opened the new airport in 1998 to facilitate tourism, and the two-story building was of a much higher quality than most of the buildings in town. Three years on, however, the airport hadn't diminished Lalibela's isolation at all. Our flight from Axum was the second of just two daily arrivals, and barely half a dozen other passengers disembarked with us. That same plane collected a few waiting passengers and departed for Bahr Dar. It was gone again before noon, and then the airport workers simply shut down the building for the day. To my disbelief, this brand-new facility had no telephones. Even the Ethiopian Airlines personnel responsible for check-in and security communicated with their office in town by two-way radio.

I needed a telephone because Tadesse's car was not waiting for us when we landed. We were a good twenty kilometers from town, and the Ethiopian Tourist Agency drivers who bundled the other arrivals into rugged four-wheel drives warned me that no more cars would come to the airport that day. I let them go on without us, and soon the place was in fact deserted. Once the building was padlocked and the airport employees gone (the airline agents by car, the porters by foot) Jean and I were alone with an inquisitive soldier in a crisp brown uniform tasked with guarding the airport (from what threats, I could not imagine). After an hour or so, we had exhausted conversation with our curious friend (where were we from? where were we going? did we have any magazines "with pictures" he could have?) and grown tired of waiting. Jean and I decided to walk toward town in the hope that we'd chance upon the odd car or truck and flag a ride up the mountain.

Except for the airport, a few huts and a cluster of low concrete buildings, the dry, open scrubland of the valley was as bare as it had appeared from the plane. Not a single tree obscured the view across the valley floor or offered shade from the blazing sun. We hiked for over an hour, until the airport building behind us looked like a child's forgotten toy, without meeting a single vehicle. Our only companions were a group of schoolchildren returning home from morning lessons. The children tagged along, peppering us with questions and giggling as they tried out rudimentary English phrases ("Hello mister how are you! Mister, you are from America mister?"). From time to time, one of them peeled off to disappear deeper into the valley or up a mountain toward homes unseen from the road.

I was beginning to wonder how we would manage the entire distance on foot when a white Land Rover finally materialized in the distance. The car rolled to a stop and a young man in an electric blue shirt and pressed gray slacks leapt out. He was Amha, the company engineer assigned to be our guide for the next day's drive. Amha practically snatched our bags from our hands as he apologized for the delay. He and the driver had met the first flight into the airport, he said, right on time. When we did not appear, they had returned to town to call the Addis Ababa office for instruction. They had then spent two hours searching fruitlessly for a working telephone—incredibly, even the telephones at the town's telecommunications center were out of order. They learned where we were only when the drivers who'd picked up the other passengers spread the word of the two tourists stranded at the airport.

Storied Lalibela looks like a place where it is perfectly possible for every telephone to be out of order. At the town's outskirts, the smooth asphalt airport road (which, I learned from Amha, my uncle had built several years earlier) crumbled into a rutted dirt strip. Along this strip, a couple of small stores, a restaurant, two or three hotels, the Ethiopian Airlines office and a series of run-down residences faced each other in uneven rows. Narrow secondary streets led to more poor construction interspersed with thirsty brown patches of ground and meager garden plots. Children, some of them just barely covered in ragged tunics, played in the road while older boys sheltered in the shade outside storefronts. Thin, dirty sheep and the occasional cow or chicken wandered freely across the streets and between the buildings. Few adults were around, and very little seemed to be happening. From the main street, I could hardly guess where the famous churches could be.

We had decided to spend that first afternoon at the church of Yemrhane Christos, one of several historic churches outside Lalibela proper. I wanted to start with Yemrhane Christos because I was intrigued by its setting—the church is concealed inside a mountain cave—and interested in its celebrated design, which mixes elements of different architectural and artistic styles and is thought to bridge the architecture of Axum and Lalibela. We stayed in town just long enough for Amha to hire one of the young men who rushed over the moment we stopped the car to guide us to the church. At his direction, we struck out in the opposite direction from the airport.

The road to Yemrhane Christos was a ruined, rocky mess. As the Land Rover, really just a simple metal frame atop four wheels, bounced mightily from bump to bump, the driver muttered crossly to himself and Amha began to eye the guide suspiciously. We, however, were too taken with the sweeping views of the Lasta mountains to mind the bumpy ride. Coming in from the airport, we'd hiked along a valley floor, looking up at the surrounding mountains. Now, we were driving along a mountain ridge and in every direction stretched mountain and valley vistas in shades of gold, yellow and pale purple, giving us a preview of the dramatic landscape to come on our tour of the company road. After about forty-five minutes, we reached a tiny collection of homes, even shabbier than those in Lalibela town (a European warehouse, presumably used for the distribution of donated food, marked the turnoff to the settlement). The driver threaded his way through the settlement and past the children who crowded around us. He stopped the car when the road came to a dead end, and from there we hiked about thirty minutes up to the mountain cave.

Yemrhane Christos was built prior to the twelfth century, but, thanks to its sheltered location, it is beautifully preserved. The church is rectangular, following the style of the earliest Ethiopian churches. Its exterior décor—rows of whitewashed stone panels and wooden beams that create a pattern of alternating luminescent white and dark brown lines broken by carved wooden windows and doors—invokes elements attributable to early Axumite architecture. Inside, every inch of the upper walls and ceiling was covered with elaborate decoration, in the manner of the churches of Lalibela and the later churches of Lake Tana. The carved and painted wood ceiling was especially dazzling: the attending deacon lit long tapers that sent candlelight dancing across intricate patterns of interwoven knots and crosses painted in bold bands of red, yellow and black.

As with the churches of Lake Tana, for me the church's setting magnified its appeal. The humidity and darkness of the cave shrouded us in a somber blanket while straw spread over olive wood flooring absorbed the sound of our steps. In dark recesses behind and on either side of the church, gleaming white human bones lay piled in exposed heaps, the remains of pilgrims who had spent their final days in the holy cave, we were told. Off to the left was a large coffin swathed in rich, elaborately woven red-and-gold fabric. Legend holds that the coffin contains the remains of Emperor Yemrhane Christos, the Zagwe king after whom the church is named. In keeping with tradition, the deacon led us in three slow, counterclockwise turns around the coffin, for the forgiveness of a chosen sin. Amha, the driver and the guide—all three of them Orthodox Christians—were silent and serious as they stepped through the matted straw, heads bent and hands clasped. I did not name a sin, or offer up a prayer, but in the damp silence I thought of the tiny settlement at the base of the mountain, the poverty of the town and the region's stark desolation, and once again, of the vast distance between my life and that of so many in Ethiopia.

The outing to Yemrhane Christos consumed what our airport adventure had left of the day, and we returned to town as night was falling. Our guide steered us to a simple motel where our room was a concrete box with a naked light bulb, a metal bed, and frayed sheets on a none-too-clean mattress (a fact we did not appreciate until we awoke with tiny red bites the following morning). Water, so scarce in the area, trickled out of rusty washroom faucets for just one hour that evening and a second hour the next morning. In the hotel restaurant, only a few of the dishes advertised on the menu were actually available. Regional farmers can barely support themselves—the area is plagued by drought and famine and is a primary source of the heart-wrenching images that the West identifies with Ethiopia. And because the town is so isolated, it does not receive reliable supplies of basic staples, much less perishables. The hotel manager offered us bread, pasta, eggs and lamb *tibs*, cubes of lamb sautéed with onions and chili peppers—the same, and the only, foods we would be offered at other restaurants and at the company camps over the next two days. My aunt had mentioned that this constant diet of bread and protein was one reason my uncle got so ill back when he spent long weeks at his project sites, but for that evening, anyway, the meal was perfect, especially since the restaurant had plenty of bottled water and cold beer on hand.

The next morning, we rose before dawn to begin our tour of the rock-hewn churches. At that early hour, as the first long fingers of morning light reached tentatively through the surrounding mountain peaks, the town was cool and perfectly still. In an old Orthodox graveyard, a few cows wandered around, grazing peacefully among weathered headstones. At the main entrance to the church complex, and in and around the churches, though, quite a few people were about. Lalibela, we were reminded, remains an important and active spiritual center for visiting pilgrims, local congregants and permanent communities of nuns and monks.

The churches of the Zagwe kings lived up to their reputation. The rays of the harsh Wollo sun that later in the day would flatten dimension and wring color from the landscape were still pale and gentle, just beginning to burn through a fine morning mist. Against this light, the massive rock edifices glowed in warm shades of ochre, creating dramatic contrasts with the mysterious, gray-black silhouettes of the interiors visible through windows and doorways cut into the stone façades in the shapes of stylized crosses or simple geometric designs. All around were the sounds and smells of early morning services: priests chanting songs while worshippers echoed their refrain, the scent of burning incense and candles drifting through the air, and the gentle rustle of clothing as standing congregants shifted their weight from side to side. We walked in and around the interconnected churches, following our guide through dark linking tunnels and narrow passageways alternating with stairways that we climbed and descended until we were quite disoriented. We peered into recesses carved into the rough, unfinished surrounding stone walls, said to be the humble homes of monks and nuns or the last resting places of pilgrims who had come to die in Lalibela. In one tiny recess a bleached human skull atop a pile of bones peered eerily back at us from the gloom. In corners and niches everywhere, monks and nuns wrapped in white cotton shawls sat bent over prayer books or lost in the ritual of worship, ignoring us as we quietly stepped past.

Tradition holds that the churches were built by King Lalibela, the most important of the Zagwe kings, a dynasty of rulers who rose to power in the ninth century. The Zagwes wrested power from the Axumite dynasty, which earned them the enduring hostility of the Orthodox clergy and many among the nobility. Historians surmise that Lalibela built the churches in his capital, known then as Roha, to demonstrate the power and religious righteousness of his dynasty and thereby undercut these critics. Whatever the Zagwes' motives, their churches were a monumental undertaking. To create them, workers first dug huge rectangular trenches into the mountains, freeing big blocks of volcanic red stone in the middle. Masons and craftsmen then chiseled these blocks from the inside and outside until they were left with free-standing buildings anchored to the living rock below. No one knows for certain whether Ethiopian craftsmen worked alone or had foreign assistance. The local legend is wonderful: it holds that God came to Lalibela in a vision and directed him to build the churches, and thereafter dispatched a host of angels to Roha every evening to complete the tasks the king's workers had begun during the day.

We were overwhelmed by massive Medhane Alem, "Savior of the World," the largest of the eleven churches at thirty-four meters long and twenty-four meters wide. The church is patterned after Axum's original St. Mary of Tsion church, perhaps a part of the Zagwe quest for legitimacy. (Pockmarks that scar the church's façade were, according to our guide, left by bullets shot at uncooperative clergy during the Italian occupation in the 1930s). The smaller Bete Maryam, "house of Mary," thought to be Lalibela's personal favorite, is intimate and charming, fronted by a moss-covered stone pool with waters said to bestow fertility on the childless women who seek the Virgin's help. Inside, there is a single, central pillar inscribed with words said to reveal the "past and future of the world." Alas, the pillar is sheathed in folds of heavy fabric and guarded by an attentive priest, so its secrets remain hidden from the casual visitor.

Finally, as the morning was beginning to brighten, we ended our visit with Bete Giyorgis, the most elegant and well-preserved of the eleven churches. Standing a bit apart from the rest of the buildings, Bete Giyorgis is shaped like a crusader's cross. Its four perfectly proportioned rectangular tines are carved down into a small plateau, rather than into the side of a mountain, so that the church's roof is at the same level as the ground around the trench in which it sits. As a result, Bete Giyorgis, which is entered by descending a steep staircase carved into the side of the trench's outer wall, can be seen in its entirety from above, its flawless geometry emphasized by the equilateral crosses chiseled into its roof as decoration. On the way back up the stairs, the guide pointed out a set of indentations in an exterior wall. These marks, he told us, were prints left by St. George's horse when the saint rode down to earth to bless the church the Zagwes built in his honor.

I was enchanted by the churches, and the magic spell cast by our morning walk through the churches might have lingered, carrying us through the rest of the day, had its hold not been shaken by Lalibela's poverty. We had already felt the region's desolation at the airport and on the drive to Yemrhane Christos; we had experienced the town's shortages of water and food in our hotel and seen that there were no bank, petrol station or businesses to speak of. Now, amidst the monoliths and adjacent monastic retreats, we encountered the extreme destitution of the villagers living near the churches. We navigated around tiny mud huts and sidestepped people squatting listlessly in dusty yards where children played with stones and sticks, unable to shake off the black flies that tormented them. As we exited through the main gate, we were besieged by alms seekers. I cannot say why, but the proximity to the solid stone churches made this manifestation of Lalibela's troubles particularly hard to witness. By the time we had worked our way back to the Land Rover, a late morning sun was glaring mercilessly down, and the town felt as dry and desolate as it had when we first drove in.

Jean and I signaled that we were ready to leave town and start the second part of the trip. Amha, who had so far been content to follow our lead, swung into action. Tadesse had decreed that we should take the company road from Lalibela all the way to its current end, near the camp at Dawunt. Amha, who was clearly proud of his role as company guide, began with a primer on the business of cutting a high-grade, all-weather gravel road through unchartered mountain terrain. In some areas the road followed old footpaths, he told us, but in most areas engineers had plotted the route after making extensive topographical and geological surveys of virgin land. Once the route was chosen, dynamiting the volcanic stone, removing rubble and maneuvering large equipment along steep mountainsides had been painstaking. The remoteness of the site had further complicated the job. Company employees remained on location for months on end, which eroded morale—Amha, who could not have been thirty, had not been to see his family in Addis Ababa in eight months. Hauling equipment and material to worksites was expensive and required weeks of advance planning. When equipment broke down, transporting mechanics and spare parts was a logistical nightmare that often resulted in long, costly delays. In dramatic illustration of Amha's words, at one point the road bit cleanly through a giant red boulder, easily fifty feet high on both sides. In ditches nearby sat the broken equipment and rusty mechanical parts sacrificed to the effort. After several hours of driving, we began to understand why the road was taking so long to build.

Amha paid particular attention to the bridges that spanned the rivers, streams, chasms and gullies along the way. At each crossing, he recited the length of the bridge, the name of the river or stream it crossed, and any special engineering problems. (Only later, after I'd spent the afternoon wondering how a young man raised in Addis Ababa could know Wollo's rivers so well, did I realize that Amha was armed with a cheat sheet he held low in his lap, invisible to me from the back seat.) The most important of these bridges was near Lalibela, a wide, white-stone arch that spanned the valley floor at the intersection of the airport road and the Addis Ababa road. The challenge for the company had been the prohibitively high cost of transporting the large stone slabs ordinarily used on bridge surfaces all the way to Lalibela. Company engineers had therefore designed and built makeshift machinery that allowed workers to mix, pour and harden the slabs right on site. Amha insisted that we scramble down the riverbank to the marshy bed below so that he could point out the special metal pins used to fasten the smaller-than-standard slabs. As Amha spoke, the ordinary concrete bridge I had barely noticed the day before came to life as an extraordinary achievement. The bridge's solidity was an uplifting contrast to the poor huts we had just seen, and I let myself hear, in Amha's animated speech, echoes of the determined kings who created the monumental churches we had just admired. Back atop the bridge, I noticed that someone had carved the company's name into the painted metal railing in neat Ethiopic characters, proudly claiming the bridge as my uncle's company's work.

Amha told us that he applied for a job with the company upon his graduation from Addis Ababa Technical College because he was impressed with its professional reputation and because of my uncle's concern for the social consequences of his business decisions. Echoing what I had heard at the marble factory, Amha spoke admiringly of Tadesse's commitment to social progress. When I remarked upon an orderly row of eucalyptus trees that hugged the outside of a wide curve, for example, Amha told me that the company tried to educate local farmers on the importance of planting and tending such trees, so that their roots would protect the road against the erosion that would otherwise, in time, destroy it. Later, Amha pointed out a section where my uncle had insisted that the road detour from its planned route and pass closer to several isolated villages, despite the additional cost to the company. The concrete buildings I had noticed near the airport were classrooms that had once been a part of a company camp; Tadesse had donated them to the town after the airport road was finished. Closer to Dawunt, where the road was still under construction, we passed men stripped to the waist clearing debris from beneath a retaining wall, and others with pickaxes hacking at a rough outcropping of stone—examples of my uncle's preference for manual labor as a way of creating jobs for local villagers.

So where did this beautiful, hard-won new road actually go? Amha sketched a map on a scrap of paper to illustrate the route from Lalibela to Woldia. As it stretched east, the road traveled through some of the most breathtaking, desolate terrain I have ever seen. It first cut through the Lasta mountain range, winding around peak after peak, descending into valleys only to ascend yet more peaks. Few signs of habitation were visible in this area, so that the splendor of the scenery was magnified by the dramatic sense of open, untouched space, spread out wide under a gray-blue sky dusted with clouds that changed both shape and shade at almost every moment. The few homes we did see were clusters of traditional thatched-roof *tukuls*. Above these homes, peasants had notched terraces of mud and stone into mountainsides to collect any drops of precious rainfall. Scruffy, low-lying bushes spaced well apart provided the only splashes of green—not even the hardy eucalyptus was much in evidence here.

Eventually, the mountain peaks and passes gave way to a wide plateau, broad enough that the mountains soon receded into the distance. This portion of the road, which continued east in a relatively flat, straight line, had been much easier to build. Here the landscape was hospitable, dotted with farmlands and one or two villages with stores, schools and even one clinic. Still, I felt a sense of desolation across the plateau almost as strong as it had been over the mountains, emphasized now by the contrast between the vivid greens of the farms and pastures and the blue of the wide flat sky.

Near the end of the plateau, the road passed through the village of Gashena, really just an intersection with a few simple buildings, where the company had until recently maintained its primary camp. Most employees had moved to the Dawunt camp as the road inched closer to Woldia, but even the modest camp that remained seemed luxurious compared to the poor villages and dwellings of the region. The camp's buildings were a mix of trailers and permanent cabins spread over about five acres encircled by a barbed wire fence. The most substantial of these structures were several well-appointed large trailers, each with two rooms, running water and hot showers, water filtration systems, and closets stocked with clean, if mismatched, linens. Upon our return from Dawunt, we stayed the night quite comfortably in one of these trailers, grateful especially for the hot shower we had not had in our Lalibela hotel room.

The final completed section of the road ran from Gash-ena to Dawunt, cutting now through the most stunning scenery of the day. A few kilometers beyond Gashena, the plateau abruptly ended, giving way to an immense canyon that sprawled between the plateau and the mountains that rose on the other side. As we descended into the canyon, the road ahead of us was like a rope lassoed around the mountain, cascading down in pale curves that appeared and disappeared until it hit the canyon bottom, where a narrow silver river snaked down the canyon bed until it too disappeared in the distance. The colors of the canyon were again the dry red and yellow hues of the morning, rendering the green of the fertile plateau a brief parenthesis. A few mountain animals were out—a fox above the road stood perfectly still, watching us intently as we went by, and a group of indigenous gelada baboons cavorted on a mountainside, quite indifferent to our presence. I'd never seen these red-bottomed, ambling creatures outside of American zoos, and I asked the driver to stop so that I could get a good look at them in this spectacular natural setting. Near the canyon bottom, as we turned a final bend, a perfect little whitewashed church popped into view. The church was another building my uncle had put up for his workers and as a gift to area villagers, whose homes were out there somewhere, hidden among the mountain peaks.

The final stretch of road, between the long low bridge across the canyon bed and the Dawunt camp, was not quite complete. Climbing this last section, we rumbled over rough surfaces not yet coated with top layers of gravel and passed groups of men at work. At one bend, men repairing a short spanning bridge waved us toward a bypass; at another, workers studying a bright yellow earthmover wedged into a ditch covered their faces against the dust the car kicked up. We were still several kilometers from the camp, and these workers seemed out of place, as if they had been airlifted in or somehow sprung forth from within the mountains.

But they were nothing compared to the surprise of the camp. Dawunt was a sprawling complex, the temporary home of nearly two hundred workers—engineers, mechanics, equipment operators, cooks, housekeepers, administrators, manual laborers. The mountains we'd just traversed had been totally empty: we had not seen any other vehicle the entire afternoon except for two trucks parked at the Gashena camp. How could so many people live and work here, in the middle of such an inhospitable terrain? The people in the camp made me think of King Lalibela's heavenly host, miraculously descended from heaven to labor on these massive mountains.

We were welcomed to the camp by Yonatan, the project manager, a heavyset man who was anxiously awaiting our arrival (Mimi, who had gotten wind of the airport delay, had made Tadesse radio the camp three times to inquire after us; a fourth call came in just after we arrived.) We thanked Amha and the driver, took a quick tour of the camp, then joined Yonatan in his trailer. We sat together for a few awkward moments—our host seemed unsure what to say to his non-engineer, relatives-of-the-boss guests. As usual, I stumbled on the proper Amharic phrases for expressing our thanks and appreciation, then volunteered a report on the day's drive. Yonatan slowly warmed to a description of the camp, the finishing touches workers were putting on the section of the road we had just driven, and the plans for the remaining few kilometers the company would build. He was not as polished or articulate as Amha, but he displayed the same pride in the road and the company's operations, as did the Gashena camp manager we were to meet later that night. Soon, the camp cooks brought us bowls of water and towels to wash up, then served us huge platefuls of *injera*, bread and lamb *tibs* with tall bottles of mineral water. We had not eaten since breakfast, and we devoured everything set before us with what must have seemed a most indecorous Western appetite.

So the road started outside Lalibela and for now stopped at Dawunt, from where it would eventually continue on to Woldia. But why was it important that this road be built? Currently, the traveler hoping to go from Lalibela to Woldia must take indirect, poor-quality secondary roads. Woldia is easily reached from Addis Ababa and points farther north, so the new road will better connect Lalibela with the rest of the country. By allowing cars into a previously inaccessible region, the road will also have a huge impact on area residents. Villagers will reach the outside world without suffering through days of travel on pack animals or on foot. And the outside world will reach the villagers more easily, so that the delivery of commercial staples and the distribution of food and other aid when needed will be faster, cheaper and safer.

These were concrete benefits, and having seen the inhospitable land between Lalibela and Dawunt, I could see why my uncle was so proud of his road. He had conquered difficult terrain despite the daunting logistics posed by a remote site and a company handicapped by a shortage of capital, equipment and trained personnel. In the process, he had made a series of secondary decisions that had helped countless people, from students and churchgoers to farmers and day laborers. I knew that it suited his independence and determination to have succeeded under such adverse circumstances, and to have done so on his own terms.

Still, I thought it ironic that far more people were gathered in the Dawunt camp than we'd seen during the entire day's journey. The region was practically uninhabited, and Lalibela itself was devoid of any economic activity aside from tourism. Whom was this road supposed to benefit? For the moment, the road stopped rather abruptly in a pile of rubble just beyond the Dawunt camp, contributing to the vague feeling that we had taken a very long drive to nowhere. If it had taken a full seven years to lay down the road between Lalibela to Dawunt, it was anyone's guess how long it would take to reach Woldia. Was this truly a good use of company energy and limited national resources? Wouldn't it be better to first focus on alleviating the deep poverty of area residents?

In the end, I think I understand why my uncle has dedicated himself to this road, and I can see the merit of the undertaking. Roads form the skeleton that supports a developing country's muscle; without decent roads, Ethiopia cannot transport goods or people from one spot to another and is stuck with regional inefficiencies. Roads, as my uncle would insist, are an investment that yields huge returns in even the remotest corners of the country. And I had already come to appreciate Tadesse's dedication to job creation, a goal well-served by such a large project. Equally important, the road also mattered for reasons that transcended straight utilitarian calculations. This road through the Lasta mountains stood for the transformative power of monuments, a power the Zagwe kings certainly understood. The road was a road, a means to get from Lalibela to Woldia. But it was also an important gesture, full of meaning for both its builders and users.

Grand projects impress, intimidate, inspire. In Ethiopia, where problems like poverty and recurring famine grind irresolvably on, the grand project may be the only undertaking that can inspire people to determined action. Poverty may never be erased, but an exquisite church or a graceful bridge can be built, and built to last. Monuments matter to builders—my uncle's sense of himself as someone who combines vision with pragmatism, for example, is gratified by his ambitious project. And monuments matter to beneficiaries and bystanders. Lalibela's churches helped legitimize the Zagwe dynasty; today those churches are a central feature of a national heritage that Ethiopians brandish like a shield against the insults of modern misfortune. Tadesse's new road may or may not become a transformative symbol (intriguingly, the road traced in places an old footpath taken by TPLF fighters on their successful 1991 march to Addis Ababa) but it is already an inspirational symbol of concrete accomplishment in a poor region of a very poor country.

Against the backdrop of Lalibela's desolation, I ultimately perceived the rock churches and the little airport and the long gravel road through the mountains as manifestations of hope and faith. Determined actors, these monuments promised, could not be stopped. When the road was finished, I imagined that my uncle, Amha, Yonatan and others would offer up a silent prayer. We have built it well, they might say, our work is complete. Now we pray that the visible fruit of our sweat and sacrifice stirs hearts and excites passions. May our toil help raise our country up once more.

Now this was a prayer in which I could join.

PART THREE
Intersections

Inside a Tukul

In all the years we lived in Ethiopia, I had only been inside one *tukul*, and that was the one on the campus of the American school I attended as a child. *Tukuls* are huts—distinctive round, mud-and-straw thatched roof homes that still dot Ethiopia's central and northern countryside. The huts are simple and a little romantic in their stylistic echo of the traditional round Ethiopian church and in their evocation of an old, rural way of life in which extended families built their homes in concentric circles around a patriarch's central hut. *Tukuls* are not, however, a feature of Addis Ababa's modern cityscape. The huts are almost always single-room structures that provide eating, living and sleeping quarters for entire families; they do not have running water and are rarely wired for electricity. They are hopelessly inconsistent with urban life and are built and used almost exclusively by the rural poor. So why did we have a *tukul* at the state-of-the-art American school in Addis Ababa? It was the classroom where the handful of Ethiopian children in each grade met for our daily Amharic language lesson.

I attended the American Community School, or ACS, for four years, from third grade through sixth. ACS was one of

several in Addis Ababa that catered to the children of dip-
lomats, missionaries and expatriate businessmen, but also
attracted local families interested in foreign language education and high academic standards. In its treatment of its Ethiopian students, ACS stood out from this group in one important respect. Unlike the British school (which I attended for
one year) or the French lyceé with their vestigial colonialism,
or the Protestant missionary schools with their antipathy to
native religion, ACS had no special notions about its Ethiopian students. To the contrary, the school was accepting of the
six to eight Ethiopian children (almost all of us the children of
professors or other professionals) in each class of about thirty,
and was almost indifferent to our status as Ethiopian nationals. As far as I remember, aside from the *tukul*, nothing about
ACS or the teachers' classroom conduct acknowledged the significant minority of non-American students, or the fact that
the campus was located in an Addis Ababa suburb. We didn't
study Ethiopian history or culture, we didn't have discussions
or projects that could have brought our personal or family circumstances into the classroom. For five out of six periods each
day, our teachers taught as if they were standing before rows
of American children in Dallas or Denver or Des Moines.

The *tukul*, the site of the sixth and special class, was the
lone marker of our difference. The little brown hut sat in the
center of a grassy courtyard, a frail organic contrast to the
solid concrete classrooms that ringed the courtyard's exterior, any of which could have been lifted from a school in
the United States. In terms of our curriculum, the Amharic
language classes were the only departure from an otherwise
ordinary school day of math, English, social studies and P.E.
And our Amharic instructor, a pudgy, spectacled man in his
early thirties, was the only Ethiopian teacher I ever had. Apart

from the hut at the center of campus and the Amharic classes conducted inside it, I cannot think of anything that was consciously "Ethiopian" about the school.

Why then the *tukul*? The answer, I think, is that even institutions that try not to differentiate among their constituents can't ignore certain basic differences. It would have been awkward for ACS, which offered its third graders French classes (taught in the regular classroom while the Ethiopian kids were in the *tukul*), not also to offer Amharic. At the same time, precisely because language is such a basic marker, providing for Amharic classes did not give too much significance to our status as Ethiopian nationals. After the language lesson was over, we were expected to fall back into a single campus community. The school's approach was a minimalist form of modern multiculturalism, which holds that it is possible to recognize and even celebrate a degree of difference and still aspire to a universalist ideal in which everyone is treated the same.

What did this mean for us, the children inside the *tukul*? Certainly, at ACS I never experienced anything like what I experienced during my year at the British school, when I was ranked third in my class each quarter, while spots one, two and four rotated among three different British students. And yet the *tukul*, literally isolated from, but surrounded on all sides by, the other classrooms, represented a most undemanding form of cultural affirmation. "Ethiopia" in this setting became a country symbolized by a quaint thatched-roof hut and not much more; the differences between Ethiopian and American students were reduced to a matter of language and little else. ACS did not otherwise depart from its broader institutional identity as an American school. The American children were not required to take Amharic classes even though the school was in Addis Ababa, while we studied Amharic in recognition of our nationality, but were otherwise expected to fit into an American framework. (Ironically, that framework also contemplated a specific idea of Ethiopia—the folkloric, "*tukul*" version—and proffered that idea to a group of urban children who felt little affinity for the huts beyond nostalgia of the sort urban Americans express when they regret the disappearance of family farms from the prairie states). ACS's approach may have been universalist, but it was not neutral or even egalitarian. Treating everyone the "same" meant, in essence, treating everyone like an American.

So ACS left us to muddle on our own through the myriad other implications of our difference and identity. We sometimes felt our difference as benign cultural chasms, as with my experience with the Girl Scouts. This after-school activity was imported to campus without a single concession to local culture. The Ethiopian girls who participated generally liked the comradery and the arts and crafts, but not one of us knew what to make of the business of earning scouting badges. We didn't understand the point of learning to start fires without matches (when could you not get matches? and what would you want to burn?), learning to tie complicated, slip-proof knots (to be used when? surely not on a *boat*), or learning how to survive several days in the woods alone (one of us, alone? and in what woods?), much less how you actually acquired these strange skills. For the most part, the only person who helped us navigate these cultural divides was our Amharic teacher. In his class, away from the American teachers and students, we admitted our confusion. How on earth, we had once wanted to know, had an upper-school teacher's brown eyes suddenly become blue? He took the time to unravel that mystery for us, to help us digest the fantastic proposition that a person could place tiny circles of colored plastic right in her eyes and still see. In this way, the lessons learned inside the *tukul* were at times as much about American culture as they were about Ethiopian language.

Other manifestations of difference were more painful. During the sixth grade, the year my parents spent in England and my last year at ACS, after-school parties suddenly became the rage among the American kids. For the Ethiopian children, ordinary social snubs over invitations (already agonizing at this age) were magnified through the prism of nationality, as we were almost never invited to these parties. Like the outsider looking in, face pressed up against a window, I decided that I had to have a party of my own. I begged and pleaded with my aunt, who absolutely hated the idea of being responsible for children whose families she did not know. Or maybe she felt uncomfortable with the idea of so many American children—I'm not sure. In any event, I was thrilled when she finally relented. I had my party one afternoon, and I didn't even care that the main event was a series of uncomfortable games that ended with clumsy kisses between the few American kids who actually came. A couple of days later, one of the American girls who hadn't come invited me to the party she was planning. Offhandedly, she remarked, "My mother said I couldn't invite any Ethiopians, except for you. You can come because you invited me to your party." I can still feel the sting of that casual comment: accustomed to thinking of myself as just myself, I was stunned to learn that others might see not me but an "Ethiopian," an unwelcome and un-American other.

But the event that truly highlighted the differences between the Ethiopian and American students—and the limitations of ACS's universalism—was the Ethiopian revolution. To this day, when I think of ACS, my first and most persistent image is of a classmate sitting alone under a tree in the playground during recess just after the death of his father, Haile Selassie's last prime minister. The Derg arrested the minister and nearly sixty other prominent figures during the first weeks of the revolution. Soon thereafter, Mengistu orchestrated hasty trials and convictions and finally, in late November of 1974, ordered the execution of the entire group.

I know this history now, and, because of the healing passage of time, I can think and write about that night as a particularly horrific link in the chain of state-sponsored violence that followed the revolution. In 1974, however, I was a frightened ten-year-old who saw these events as they were reflected in the clouded mirrors of a classmate's eyes. The prime minister's son missed weeks of school after his father's death, and when he returned, he was a different boy. Each day during recess, he would walk over to the same tree and sit alone under its shelter, looking off into the distance until the bell rang us back inside. I knew what had happened to his father, and later on, I am sure he knew what happened to mine, but we did not speak of these horrors. We felt fear, loss and isolation, and sensed the same in each other, but we did not know how to express our feelings or to comprehend the revolution's meaning.

Under different circumstances or in a different (Ethiopian) school, the revolution would have seeped into every moment of our day, but ACS left us to ourselves even then. Our teachers rarely referred to the coup or the Derg and never acknowledged the specific situation of any one student. We had no discussion about my classmate's sudden silence or about what we should do in response; later, when my father was arrested, my teachers did not acknowledge his plight or offer me much comfort. In the classroom, with our teachers and even with each other, the Ethiopian students acted as if the revolution stopped at the campus gates. And yet each one of us under-stood that the revolution would have dramatic repercussions for us that our American classmates would not experience. We could not observe events in our city with the detachment of the expatriate, as our teachers and classmates could. We could no longer assume the permanence of our lifestyles or even our safety, because we had seen the revolutionary flames burst through our protective compound walls. And we did not imagine we could pack up and leave when the city got too dangerous, for Addis Ababa was the only home we knew.

We had only the *tukul*, that traditional and imperfect shel-ter, to shield some small part of us from the storm.

* * *

Back in Addis Ababa, Jean and I visited a second *tukul*. This was the Crown Hotel, a new restaurant off the Debre Zeit road that offered a wonderful buffet of Ethiopian dishes and nightly performances of traditional dances from across the country. To showcase the food and entertainment, the owners had housed the restaurant inside an oversized *tukul*. Like the ACS classroom, the restaurant was a setting for a specific acknowledgement of difference, this time the differ-ences among those within Ethiopia.

The restaurant was very popular. By the time we arrived, at around eight o'clock one weeknight, the muddy parking lot was full and we had to leave our cars in a far corner and pick our way back to the front door through puddles left by an afternoon shower. A friendly host ushered us through an outer foyer and into the large round main room where he seated us at a low table with benches and handmade wooden stools. Half the room was set with tables, almost all already occupied by noisy groups of Ethiopians, other Africans and Westerners. The other half of the room was open, and in that semicircle was a trio of musicians who played both traditional and modern instruments. Off to one side were the buffet tables, watched over by attentive waiters who kept the steaming platters full. Beautiful young women in colorful *shemma* dresses stepped lightly from table to table, urging guests to the buffet and taking orders for beer and *tej* and soft drinks. Above our heads, thick wooden beams came together like spokes to form the *tukul*'s roof; sheaves of long brown grass bound with wire filled in the spaces between the beams.

We had just enough time to order drinks and fill our plates before a group of six men and women filed out a side door to the left of the band and the dances began. The performances were lively, absorbing and instructive. Many, even most, of the dances were new to me—I can just barely do the *iskista*, the hands-on-waist, shoulder-shaking dance of Amharic and Tigrinya speakers—so I was happy to watch the men and women perform in their colorful clothing and headdresses. Our hosts for the evening, friends of Mimi and Tadesse, described different facets of the dances, eager that we understand and enjoy the spectacle before us. Around us, other Ethiopian hosts were doing the same, whispering and pointing out details to their tablemates. The atmosphere was warm and festive—people were out to enjoy themselves. A house photographer worked the room, taking souvenir snapshots of groups gathered at tables. Between dances a table of American women with flushed faces rose to pose with the musicians.

So what was the meaning of this *tukul*? As with the Amharic classes at ACS, I think the conscious idea behind the performances was a simple desire to acknowledge and celebrate Ethiopia's many cultures. At this level, the evening was an innocuous, pleasurable exploration of different dances. What got complicated, to my mind, was the relationship between the dancers and the audience and the dissonance between cultural difference as it was displayed inside the *tukul,* and difference as it is actually playing out in Ethiopia today.

Ethiopia is a highly diverse country—its seventy-five million inhabitants, for example, speak over eighty distinct languages. To me, the depth of this diversity underscores the poignancy of a night of quaint folkloric dance, in which audiences are entertained, but not engaged. Many of Ethiopia's smaller linguistic and ethnic groups are dying out or assimilating into larger groups, victims of demographic trends, modernization and land-use policies. Of these eighty languages, only a handful—Amharic, Orominya, Tigrinya, Gurage, Somali and a few others—are likely to survive more than a generation or two.

Sitting in the restaurant, absorbed by the lively performances, it was possible to believe for the duration of an evening that the culture and the groups represented on stage remain a vibrant and integral part of the national landscape. But marginalization and loss are on the rise and in time the cultures and artifacts of these peoples will be seen only in museums and in staged performances. The makeup of the audience was telling: the Ethiopians in the room were all Westernized urbanites, not one of whom was wearing traditional clothing. Between mouthfuls of *injera* and sips of *tej,* guests could dip their toes in a sparkling pool of "national" culture despite the muddy truth that modern Addis Ababa, at least, reflects very little of that cultural diversity.

The performances also served up culture in helpings that left out the complex questions of identity and affiliation that cultural differences inevitably raise. The evening's entertainment implied the existence of an agreed model of national coexistence, of tolerance among citizens who trusted each other to value their respective cultures without threatening the nation itself. Each dance was given equal billing by the performers, each was presented with equal skill and enthusiasm, and each received equal audience attention and applause, all in a warm, receptive atmosphere. Call it, once again, a minimalist form of modern multiculturalism, whose adherents believe that differences are important but never paramount, significant, but always subservient to national affiliation.

But it isn't at all clear that this is the model Ethiopia is pursuing, as even I had felt during my short stay in Axum. On the contrary, the linguistic, ethnic and religious lines that run through Ethiopia today are live wires, and people are struggling to define both the content and significance of the categories they demarcate. What does it mean to call oneself an Amhara or an Oromo? Do people experience those categories as distinct or overlapping? What is the significance of the line between Amharic-speaking and Tigrinya-speaking Orthodox Christians? If the categories are distinct and meaningful, is it possible—or even desirable—to pursue a multiethnic nation in which groups coexist peacefully and respectfully and without challenging the nation's unity? Or do ethnic and linguistic identities trump national identity, so that the country itself is at risk?

These questions are both serious and unsettled. The debates begin with the uncertain topography of history: political leaders, academics and others do not agree on the role that ethnicity or language played in Ethiopia's past. On the one hand are those who maintain that the Amharas ruled the country at the expense of all other groups; on the other are those who counter that while Amharic may have been the language of the imperial court, the country's elite, including its kings and queens, were people who came from all regions of the country. The latter group believes that Ethiopia's ethnic groups are suspect categories, as migration patterns and intermarriage have blurred the lines that separate them and created a polyglot citizenry; the former dismisses this claim as the convenient belief of a group trying to preserve its historical advantage.

For its part, the current government has adopted policies that have prompted Ethiopians to become more conscious than ever of their ethnic and linguistic backgrounds. The government may be pursuing these policies because it genuinely feels there are inequities to be corrected. Or it may be doing so because it is largely made up of Tigrean leaders who first came together to fight for the independence of Tigre province and such policies, especially to the extent they drive a wedge between Amharic and Orominya speakers, are an effective way to advance the interests of Tigrinya speakers. Whatever the rationale, the policies promote ethnic identities at the expense of a national identity and pit groups against one another by stressing differences and reigniting old conflicts.

For example, the government has abandoned the old province system and drawn up nine new administrative regions or *"killils"* defined and administered by whatever linguistic or ethnic group is in the majority in the region. Instead of Shoa, Wollo, Bale and Arussi, there are now the *killils* of Amhara, Oromia and Tigre. When Jean and I were in Bahr Dar to tour the churches of Lake Tana, we happened upon a squat concrete block of a building with a sign proclaiming it the center of the Amhara administrative region. If I must label my family, I suppose it is nominally Amhara, but I doubt any one of us feels particularly connected to Bahr Dar over, say, the town of Nazareth, my paternal grandparents' home, in the heart of the region designated as Oromo, or over a town like Axum, in the Tigre region, where Ethiopian history was born. The government's policies are painful to Ethiopians who see themselves as connected to the entire country, rather than to a single region, and especially hard on people whose roots or current home are within a region designated for another group. We heard plenty of stories about minority farmers and small business owners feeling immense pressure to sell their land or businesses to members of the local majority and about parents struggling with schools that conduct classes only in Orominya or Tigrinya. And the *killil* system of nine regions does nothing to address the minority status of Ethiopia's seventy-one other liguistic groups.

For me, this is a hard debate to enter after so many years abroad. It is clear that if Ethiopians feel or are made to feel their linguistic and ethnic differences as identities that trump their national identification, it will become increasingly hard to defend and preserve the multicultural nation. Already, ethnicism has led to separatist violence in the Oromo regions of southern Ethiopia and in the Ogaden region that is home to a large population of Somalis; ethnicism was, of course, the driving force behind Eritrean secessionism. And these conflicts and government policies (and the evening's performance) do not even address the line that has most divided Ethiopia over the centuries: the line between Christian and Muslim. Religious division has been at the root of the country's bloodiest internal clashes and could, in an atmosphere where a national identity takes a backseat to linguistic, regional or other identities, easily come to pose the most serious challenge yet to the national project. I dread to think what the rise of radical Islam in neighboring countries—in Sudan, in Somalia, even in Eritrea—could mean if this ancient fault line creaks back to life.

As these battles rage on within Ethiopia, global tides are steadily wearing at the nation from without. Addis Ababa looks more Western each day; the city's elite speak English and wear the latest American styles; national culture thrives best on stage before an international audience. Sometimes, even internal cultural struggles are resolved in ways that will ultimately hurt national culture vis-à-vis external forces. I was saddened to hear of the debate over whether to write Orominya, historically a spoken language, in Roman letters rather than the letters of the indigenous Ethiopic script in which Amharic and Tigrinya are written. Whatever problems Oromo speakers may have had or still have with Amharic and Tigrinya speakers, Ethiopia's indigenous script is a unique cultural treasure. If Orominya, the second most widely spoken language, is written in Roman letters, I think that it will be a loss for all of Ethiopia.

* * *

In the end, I am not quite sure what to make of difference in Ethiopia.

I went to visit my old school, of course, and found the little *tukul* in its spot at the center of campus, still there after all these years. I was surprised at first, but on reflection I could not think of any reason why the school would have changed the way it teaches its Ethiopian students. The experience of difference is highly personal, and others may not agree, but my own sense is that, all in all, ACS did not do us any lasting harm. We chose the school for the good education, and if as a by-product of that education we had to struggle to fit our Ethiopian selves into an American universalism, at least that struggle was limited by the scope of our school day. We all came from relatively privileged families, we were not minorities in the city and society beyond the school compound, and Ethiopia was not burdened with a colonial past. We did not face the condescension or outright discrimination that marked institutions like the British school; moreover, almost any form of overt multiculturalism would have raised questions like those raised by a night of benign folkloric dance. As far as I know, my former classmates have been quite successful in the adult paths they have chosen and it is my assumption that our early schooling contributed to that success. ACS could have served us better, but its shortcomings were not fatal. I'm now betting that the *tukul* will be there as long as the school remains in business, and I can't see why that is such a bad thing.

As for differences among Ethiopians, perhaps I cannot shake off my Amhara background of supposed privilege; perhaps my views are a result of my early years at ACS and my many years in the multicultural United States; perhaps I'm too much my father's daughter. Again, I recognize that the experience of ethnic or racial or linguistic difference is highly personal, and that I cannot know what others feel on this score. Still, I do not believe that Ethiopia and Ethiopians are better off divided along ethnic or other lines, in the form of government-mandated *killils* or autonomous regions or independent states. At a time when other countries are drawing closer together to pool economic resources, I cannot believe that Eritrea with its tiny population and arid deserts is better off without Ethiopia, or that a landlocked Ethiopia is better off without Eritrea and the Red Sea coast. I dread to think that Ethiopia might follow the logic of ethnicity to the point where the country shatters into so many ethnically homogenized *killils*. Africa is sick with examples of such disintegration; in each case the divided country's problems have only deepened, leaving millions in trouble and a rapacious few enriched.

The balances that multiethnic countries strike between cultural accommodation on the one hand and national unity on the other are flawed and prone to internal contradictions. But I fear these imperfections a lot less than I fear the dissolution of the nation, and recent opposition to TPLF policies indicates that many Ethiopians believe a healthy balance can be struck. So I leave ACS, the Crown Hotel and Ethiopia, hoping that a national commitment to linguistic and ethnic recognition within the borders of a unified country can blossom beyond the warm, easy circle of a *tukul*.

Outside an Embassy

After a stop at nearby Medhane Alem church so that she can pray for my success, Mimi drops me off near the main entrance of the American embassy, in front of a row of thick, waist-high concrete barricades. As I get out of the car, an Ethiopian security guard strides over, a frown on his face. For a moment, he and I look each other over with the assurance that comes with just a little bit of power relative to others: he has a job at the American embassy, not to mention a large gun, whereas I am armed with that magical blue passport, coveted throughout the Third World. The guard begins to berate me for having been dropped off so close to the embassy entrance—apparently cars are forbidden to stop anywhere along the length of the concrete barricades. Feeling both defiant (to hell with his intimidation) and a little guilty (my confidence comes from my citizenship, and where is the pleasure in flaunting that good fortune to a guard just doing his job?), I ignore his tirade and make a show of waving my passport at him. His frown deepens, but he lets me pass. I cut in front of a long, listless line of waiting people and duck through the entrance.

I am at the embassy to help my aunt Itiyobia get a visa to travel to the United States. Itiyobia—whose name means

"Ethiopia"—is my father's older sister, the person to whom he was closest as a child and young man. She shares with him a distinct set of experiences that form the basis of their close relationship, experiences that are so distant in time and place it is nearly impossible for me to imagine them. When, for example, my father describes traveling from the tiny village of Shenkora to the nearest town at the age of eighteen to use a telephone for the first time, I struggle to visualize the rural Ethiopian villages of the 1930s and 1940s in which the two of them came of age. When he tells me about the grandfather who died on the battlefield, I try to imagine what such young children must have felt as they watched him march off to fight the Italians, or how they experienced the five long years of Italian occupation. When he matter-of-factly describes how my grandmother, a free spirit, left my grandfather several times over the course of their marriage to live with other men, I do my best to conjure the pain of abandonment he and Itiyobia must have felt. In each case, I know that I fall short. Through these circumstances (and more that I cannot know) he and Itiyobia, and no one else, lived together.

My father is now 73, and Itiyobia is 77. The two of them have not seen each other since we left Ethiopia, and for my father the separation from his sister is one of the most painful results of his separation from his country. He of course has not been able to return to Ethiopia, and Itiyobia, who has never traveled far from Addis Ababa, and does not speak English, has not had the resources to undertake the long journey to the United States.

A few months before my trip home, my father had finally persuaded Itiyobia that she could and should make the trip. Time, he had argued pointedly, was working against them. So Itiyobia had gathered up her documents, gotten her first passport and applied for a tourist visa. To our surprise, the embassy had twice turned her down. Over the years the American consul has granted many in my family tourist and even immigrant visas, so we decided the denials must have stemmed from some lack of documentation. My parents hoped that if I, with my fluent English and legal education, spoke directly with a consular official, I could resolve any problems and clear the way for an approval.

I reunited with Itiyobia over lunch at Mimi and Tadesse's house the first day we were in Addis Ababa. My aunt seemed just as I remembered her—the intervening years had not changed her much. She is not at all beautiful in a classic sense: she is heavy, with the round face that both she and my father inherited from my grandmother, and gray hair that gathers in a wiry cloud around her head. But her skin is smooth and dewy, and her face radiant in the way of certain older women who shoulder their hardships with both grace and resignation. She is serious in her bearing, and dresses always in a simple *shemma* dress and matching *netela* draped loosely over her shoulders. She does not have children, and still lives in the same modest wooden house she has rented since I was a child. I'd always assumed she had never married, and learned only on this trip that she had in fact been widowed at a young age.

I knew, of course, that getting Itiyobia a visa mattered a lot to my parents, but by the end of that first meal the challenge became mine as well. The very first thing Itiyobia wanted to know was why I was in Ethiopia at all. She had convinced herself that none of us would ever return unless something was wrong with the family and with my father in particular. My father's arrest and injury remain for her a fresh and painful memory, perhaps because her images of him from the difficult period of our departure have not been supplanted by

images of his recovery and life in the United States. Just seeing me and talking about my family upset her, and I saw tears
in her eyes more than once that afternoon. I was touched by
her affection and concern, and gently tried to remind her of
what she already knew—that we were safe, that my father
was physically stable and professionally productive, that his
children had settled into their lives in America—and to assure
her that I was there only to visit family and country after
many years. She seemed satisfied, and we eventually settled
into easy conversation with others as we ate. Then, during a
pause in the conversation, she abruptly pointed down at my
sandaled feet.

"Take off your shoe," she said.

"Excuse me, *Tye* Itiyobia?" I thought I had misheard her.

"Take off your shoe," she repeated. The explanation, such
as it was, came a beat later: "I want to see my brother's foot."

My father's foot? But as Itiyobia's tone did not invite discussion, I swallowed the question and slipped off my right
sandal. For a long moment the two of us examined my bare
foot. I was glad I did not have to meet her eyes just then,
because I needed a minute to absorb the sentiment behind her
request. Sharing a sofa with me at lunch was the closest Itiyobia had come to my father in twenty-five years, and I realized
that she was searching out every trace of him in me.

"My feet are so funny-looking," I said, finally. "Don't you
think they look like rectangles?" It was all I could think of to
say, just words to help check the emotion brought on by the
idea that this faint physical echo of my father could somehow
ease the pain of her separation from him.

When I raised the question of going to the embassy on
her behalf a few days later, Itiyobia protested. She hated the
idea of contact with authority, even an American authority,

because she thought all institutions were endless sources of trouble. She feared that just by appearing at the embassy, I might somehow trigger a chain of unwelcome events for myself or my father. Moreover, having been denied twice, she didn't think the officials would change their minds. I insisted that I should try. I reminded her that I was now an American, adding lightly that the embassy was "mine," there to help me with whatever I needed. Mimi, who (although she shared Itiyobia's pessimism) did not want me to leave Addis Ababa before I had done everything my parents had requested, chimed in with her support. Finally, Itiyobia reluctantly agreed to let me go.

The American embassy sits inside a large, imposing stone compound up the Entoto mountain road. My initial taste of the embassy came on our first day's tour of the city, when Tadesse drove Jean and me up Entoto road to point out the compound and the Medhane Alem church. Afterwards, wanting to return to the city below, Tadesse made a U-turn just beyond the embassy compound. As we turned around, one of the guards at the entrance began shouting at us and yelled at us to pull over. Waving his arms at Tadesse, he barked out that U-turns—never mind that we were in a public street— were not permitted in front of the embassy. Although we were now facing the other direction, the guard insisted that we turn around again and continue up the mountain road. Rolling his eyes but long past arguing in such situations, Tadesse had complied and found another route back into the city.

The guard's insistence that we turn around had been an irksome show of petty power, but neither that first encounter nor my exchange with the guard at the entrance the day of my trip, worried me too much. I hoped that once I cleared all such peripheral hurdles, I would eventually meet a rational person who would agree that there could be no harm in allowing an elderly woman to visit her elderly brother in the U.S. The American embassy had often been difficult to deal with, but it had never actually let my family down.

Once inside the embassy's main entrance, I passed through metal detectors and heavy security doors and had my passport checked by two sets of personnel, and then found myself alone in a small room. For a moment I couldn't figure out where I was supposed to go—I was a bit startled at being alone at all, given the layers of security I had just negotiated. I noticed on one wall a poster of the type commonly seen in fast-food restaurants, identifying the "employee of the month." This month, the American embassy was honoring a security guard as its top employee.

Spotting a small sign marked "American citizens," I exited the room into a deserted courtyard, followed a paved walkway to another building and climbed a flight of external stairs. At the top of the stairs, I opened a metal door and to my surprise stepped directly into a windowless room absolutely packed with people. I didn't exactly expect a private chamber where consular officials would receive American citizens, but neither did I expect to be in a room full of visa-seekers. The room was drab, unadorned except for an American flag and (long after the election of George W. Bush) a portrait of President Bill Clinton, plus bulletin boards papered with forms and miscellaneous notices. ("Danger! American citizens are warned of recent bandit activity in the Southern Nile Valley area.") Several rows of plastic chairs faced a wall of glass booths, and in one corner an empty water dispenser stood near a trashcan overflowing with crumpled paper cups. Anxious people dressed in Sunday-best clothes waited in quiet groups, tensing each time a name was called out over the PA system. The scene was familiar to me from my own visits to Western embassies and INS offices before I became a U.S. citizen. My heart sank.

A separate booth at the far end of the room was labeled "For American Citizens." Gathering myself, I asked the young Ethiopian woman at the booth for a citizen registration form—a way for the embassy to keep track of Americans visiting Ethiopia and a way for me to see embassy officials in action before revealing what I really wanted. The woman was polite enough, and when she called my name to return my passport, I told her that I also wanted to discuss a relative's visa application. She took Itiyobia's file and warned me that it might be some time before a consular official could see me. I sat down to wait with everyone else.

While I waited, I watched two consular officials, both African-American women in their mid-50s, efficiently dispense with applicants. Because the room was so quiet, I could hear every word between the women behind the glass and the anxious people at the booths. With each exchange, I grew increasingly worried. The applicants were not all sympathetic, but the two women made the guards outside seem downright gracious.

The first exchange involved a well-dressed middle-aged woman seeking a tourist visa. The consular official accused the woman of having previously overstayed a visa that had been stamped into another passport. The woman vehemently denied this accusation.

"I have never traveled abroad before—never in my life! Of course I do not have another passport!" she insisted.

But the official apparently had hard evidence of the woman's earlier travels. Behind her stood (not sat) an Ethiopian translator, and I listened as the translator struggled to convey the Americanisms the frustrated official began shouting through the glass:

"Tell her that if she doesn't stop lying I'll put a note in her file and then she'll never ever get the hell out of Dodge!"

Every aspect of this exchange was deflating—the relationship between the seated American official and the standing Ethiopian translator, the official's rudeness, the woman's patent lies that surely made it that much harder for the next applicant to get a fair hearing.

Another exchange involved a winner in the diversity visa lottery that the United States had recently opened to residents of under-represented countries. Lottery winners must find financial sponsors in the U.S., and then must wait forever before their "right" to immigrate is cleared. Still, winning the lottery is considered a stroke of incredible luck. Winners can immigrate permanently to the U.S., and they have the right to immigrant visas for spouses and children. This right, it turns out, has become, reportedly, a source of fraud, as winners enter into sham marriages so they can get visas for friends or relatives. I watched a thin young man in an oversized suit get into a shouting match with the official about whether the woman with him was his wife, as he claimed, or his sister, as the official apparently believed. In broken English he kept shouting, "This is not the America only I am meaning here! You are insulting me! This is my future! This is for me and my wife my future in the America!" Eventually, the couple sat down, and eventually got up again and left the room.

And so it continued. Very few people seemed happy with their results.

Finally, I saw one of the consular officials confer briefly with the woman stationed at the American citizens' booth. A moment later my name was called. Heart beating, I walked slowly across the room. Before coming to the embassy, I had studied Itiyobia's folder and prepared for a persuasive exchange about why the embassy should grant her a visa. I quickly ran through the facts in my head one last time. Itiyobia's documents were in order, neatly assembled in her file. She had included the requisite information about her family members, local assets and other ties to Ethiopia. She had appended an affidavit from one of my cousins stating that she would pay all of Itiyobia's expenses while Itiyobia was in the U.S. She had included a letter from my father's doctors explaining why he can't travel to Ethiopia to visit her, a letter the embassy officials requested when they first reviewed her application. Again, the embassy had granted tourist visas to other elderly members of my family, including both my grandmothers, all of whom had returned to Ethiopia. Why should it now refuse Itiyobia? I didn't expect a change of mind on the spot, but I did expect the official to review the file and to discuss with me what Itiyobia should add to win a positive response.

The consular official was waiting for me behind the partition. The Ethiopian woman had vacated her chair for her, but she hadn't taken it. I could see Itiyobia's closed folder on the counter, beneath a pair of manicured hands.

The official spoke before I could. "Yes. What is the problem here?" she asked, barely glancing up at me.

"Uh—hello, ma'am." I was a little flustered by her brusque opening. "How are you. I'm—I'm here to ask about my aunt's, my father's sister's, application for a visa."

"And?"

And? I had just seen her confer with the Ethiopian woman so I knew she knew exactly why I was here. I took a deep breath and tried to banish my nerves from my voice.

"Well, ma'am, as you surely know, my aunt was denied. She didn't get a visa. So I'd like to find out—my family would like to know—why that happened, because we think that her file is complete and—"

"The consul can grant or deny visas at its discretion," she interjected, again without looking up.

"Yes, of course you have that right, I know that. I've come here because my family wants to understand how you came to that decision. This visa is very important to us, and we want to provide you with whatever information you would like so that —"

Again, I was cut off. This time, the consul held up her right palm to signal that she was no longer listening and with her left hand she pushed a slip of paper beneath the glass partition. I looked down and saw the legal standard for reviewing visa applications printed in capital letters: the American consul can grant or deny tourist visas at its discretion, and will deny them if it feels the applicant has not presented adequate evidence of an intent to return to the country of origin.

I tried again. "Yes, ma'am, I understand the legal standard. I came here because my family is hoping to get guidance from you on what my aunt should do to satisfy the standard."

"The consul can grant or deny a visa at its discretion," she repeated impatiently.

"Yes, I'm a lawyer, I understand that. But can you please help us understand what we can do to show you that my aunt has no intention to stay in the United States? We can provide anything, more letters, whatever you need."

It was hard to speak through the glass, hard to gauge whether I was having any impact. I tried to emphasize the personal.

"This is very important to my family," I said. "My father can't come to Ethiopia, and he hasn't seen his sister for twenty-five years. And they are both getting old now."

"All I can tell you is that this lady is free to apply again."

"But—but you've said no twice, and we want to make sure we give you whatever you need so that she gets a better answer next time. My aunt's whole life is here in Ethiopia. She'd never stay in the States."

"Yes, I'm sure."

"I think that if you met her, and interviewed her, you would see that."

"I already said, she can apply again." Her voice was flat and final.

"But is there more we can do to satisfy your concerns? Other members of my family have come to visit and they have always come back. What can we add to the file?"

"Look, I don't care what you do," the consul finally snapped, looking me squarely in the eyes for the first time. "As far as I am concerned, this lady can apply again and again. She can fill out that form and apply a million times if she wants. Be my guest."

With that, she gave Itiyobia's folder a dismissive little tap, then turned and disappeared into the offices on her side of the glass. As I stared blankly at her back, the Ethiopian woman, who had discreetly listened to our exchange, apologetically slid Itiyobia's folder back under the partition.

I was shocked and absolutely humiliated. I had been turned down in an exchange that lasted less than five minutes and in which the official showed no respect for me, no empathy for my father or Itiyobia, not the slightest regret about refusing us. I returned slowly to my seat, my face burning. Now that the consul had turned me away, I realized just how much I had expected to succeed. It didn't matter that so many other applicants had been turned down—I had believed that I would prevail, for all the reasons I am generally successful in my life: I am educated, articulate, resourceful, not poor, and now American. These attributes separate me from my aunt, and I rely on them to my benefit nearly every day. When the consular official refused me and walked off, these elements of my identity faded and I felt myself dissolve into the unhappy Ethiopian crowd. Like everyone around me, I despaired in the knowledge that I was powerless to appeal her decision, no matter how arbitrary the denial or how proper the request.

And of course, I was not the real subject of this story. I was angry that the official had treated me so poorly, but in the end what did her manners matter? For me—part Ethiopian, part American—the trip to the embassy was a biting reminder that power is often exercised arbitrarily, and that the lawyer's tools that equip me to fight back in America mean little in an embassy in Ethiopia. For Itiyobia—female, single, childless, elderly, poor, black, African, so much a symbol of the country after which she is named—the outcome held little surprise. Itiyobia must swallow arbitrary decisions in a world in which the odds are stacked against her, and she does not expect to come out on top.

* * *

I had already said goodbye to Itiyobia before my trip to the embassy. At our parting, she had two gifts for me. First, she gave me an oversize *netela* with a beautiful orange border, remarking that the large shawls were ideal for strapping infants to the back. She said this matter-of-factly, assuming the right of older family to speak on such matters, and without pausing for my reaction. For some reason, I wasn't bothered by her comment, even though I had always been a little annoyed when others brought up the subject of children.

I loved the idea that some future American child might be linked to this loving Ethiopian great-aunt through this pretty piece of cloth, and accepted the gift with pleasure.

Then, taking her wallet from her handbag, Itiyobia carefully removed a small photograph of my father that he had sent her during his first year of study abroad, at the American University in Cairo, in 1951. My father wouldn't have been much older than seventeen or eighteen at the time the photo was taken, and I'd never seen a photograph of him at this age. I studied it for a long time, but I couldn't recognize the serious young man peering out of the old black-and-white shot. I was deeply moved that Itiyobia wanted me to have a photograph she had carried with her for over fifty years, but I could not accept the gift. The faded image made me see again that Itiyobia/Ethiopia knows my father in ways that no one else, not even my mother, can ever know him. I could not take from her this cherished memento when the time and history of which it spoke were so far outside my knowledge and comprehension and so much a part of hers. Touched by the affection behind her offer, I pressed the photo back in her hand.

Going to the embassy was the most frustrating, and the saddest, moment of my trip to Ethiopia. I so wanted to succeed, so wanted to have a hand in bringing Itiyobia and my father together again. The only thing that cheers me up at all when I think of the episode is knowing that my father will never accept the idea that he simply cannot see his sister again. He will cajole Itiyobia into applying for a visa again, again and again, just as the consular official so rudely suggested. And who knows? There is no reason—by definition—why an arbitrary no can't one day become an arbitrary yes. Some afternoon up on Entoto mountain, maybe even Itiyobia's luck will turn.

Claiming a Country

"Habesha nat! Ere habesha aydelechim! Ishe isti annegagrat!"
On the streets of Gondar, Lalibela and Bahr Dar, occasionally even in Addis Ababa, I attracted groups of schoolchildren who wanted to know what I was. Perhaps it was my dress and casual hair, perhaps it was that I was alone with a *ferenji* man, perhaps it was my very stride and bearing.

"She is Ethiopian! No, she isn't! Okay, I dare you, you talk to her!" the children chattered as they inched closer to me for a better look.

They reminded me of my seventh-grade social-studies teacher in Cold Spring, Minnesota, who, during a unit on nationality and citizenship, once placed his hand atop my head and asked, "Class, what is Haile?" (Answer: an alien.) I would listen to the children debate me for a bit, translating for Jean's amusement, then turn, address them in Amharic and watch them scatter in a burst of screams and good-natured giggles.

As I had made my plans to go back to Ethiopia, I was preoccupied with the question of whether and how I, now

American, would fit in. I worried that my limited Amharic, my lack of religiosity, my unfamiliarity with local customs and my American upbringing would leave me stranded at the edge of Ethiopian society. I had imagined that I would be an awkward outsider and readied myself for uncomfortable, frustrating or even offensive interactions. Focused as I was on my own perspective and my own feelings, it didn't even occur to me to ask the related question. That is, might Ethiopia also be trying to make sense of people like me, her departed sons and daughters? Might the country we had left be just as concerned about its reception of us?

I was right to expect awkward moments, but I learned also that the thousands of immigrants displaced by the revolution have begun to change Ethiopia. During my stay, I was struck again and again by the ways in which Ethiopia and Ethiopians were struggling to understand—and, at times, to accommodate—me and others who now bridge the divides that separate those who "belong" to Ethiopia from those who do not. The curious children of the northern villages could not agree on whether I was one of them, and I don't know whether my few words of Amharic settled their debates. But what was clear, and significant, was that something about me made the children question, if just for a few lighthearted moments, their idea about what makes a person Ethiopian. That was the surprising discovery: that I and other returning immigrants have begun to urge such questions on the people and institutions we had left behind. Once asked, moreover, the questions are often—not always, but often—answered in ways that accommodate and include us.

I experienced efforts to make sense of me in encounters with people from Addis Ababa to Axum. Most receptive, of course, were family and friends, the people predisposed to embrace me no matter how much I'd strayed from their ideas of what constitutes a proper Ethiopian woman. I know that my grandmother and my aunt Itiyobia find me strange—why didn't I wear a cross or go to church? Why, at the time of my visit, was I thirty-six and childless?—yet it would never occur to them to deny my Ethiopianness, to consider me any less a part of our family than any other grandchild or niece. Similarly, Mimi, who was most involved with our day-to-day activities, acquiesced to requests I know she considered inappropriate. She did not want me to travel outside Addis Ababa without the protection of the official Ethiopian tourist agency; she did not want me to spend an evening alone in Tadesse's office; she refused to let me drive her car to the Hilton Hotel where I wanted to take Jean for a drink one evening. I chalked her reluctance up to Ethiopian conservatism about women and grumbled to Jean that this was one reason I could never live in the confines of Addis Ababa. But then Mimi's resistance crumbled under the great weight of her desire to make me happy. Reluctantly, she helped us make our independent travel plans, though upon our return from Bahr Dar she hugged me longer and harder than she had when I first arrived in Ethiopia. She eventually agreed that I could manage alone in Tadesse's office and graciously said nothing about what might have befallen me during the blackout. And though she could not bring herself to hand over her car keys (her compromise was to make Tadesse take us), I think she understood that the reason I did not press her was out of respect for her, and not because I agreed with her ideas about appropriate female behavior.

It may be relatively easy to let affection draw a curtain over a granddaughter's lack of faith or permit a visiting niece some freedoms during her month-long stay. But I am sure

that a longer trip would have precipitated more serious chal-
lenges. This point was made clear to me on the morning Mimi
and I stopped to have coffee with T—, the neighbor who had
called Mimi's home to report that soldiers were surrounding
our house on that October afternoon. T—'s daughter, a childhood friend and fellow ACS student, now lives in Washington
D.C. with her African-American husband. When we entered
the parlor of T—'s modest house, I noticed the framed photos
of her daughter, son-in-law and grandchildren on her shelves
and my stomach tightened. So many Ethiopians believe themselves superior to the darker-skinned peoples of sub-Saharan
Africa—in fact, many don't even consider themselves black—
and anti-African racism is both deeply ingrained and ubiquitous. Just a day or two earlier I had watched another relative
think nothing of casually shouting a terrible epithet at a char-
coal-skinned farmer whose flock of sheep blocked her car,
and even among immigrants living in the U.S. the sentiment
is common. I find this racism painful to witness and hard to
confront—I'd cringed but said nothing in the car that afternoon. So when T— reached for the photographs, I put down
my coffee cup and braced myself, wondering if I would find
the courage and the right words to object to the conversation
I was sure I would hear.

To my surprise, neither T— nor my aunt said anything
remotely objectionable. Instead, T— spoke at length about
how wonderful the husband is, how hardworking, how kind,
how loving ("He was so warm on my very first visit, truly, he
was nothing like a *ferenji*"). As I slowly let down my guard, I
thought to myself that T—'s enthusiasm reflected more than
the boasts of a proud mother. She also meant to counter the
reservations she assumed that Mimi and I harbored, and it was
all I could do to stop myself from jumping up and hugging her

for her concern. Of course cultural accommodation driven by maternal love is not a sure sign of broader change afoot, but at a minimum T—'s embrace of her son-in-law affects the people around her. I left her house elated to think that even a cultural burden as heavy as Ethiopian racism can be lightened through the actions of immigrants who've rejected it.

Beyond the realm of familial and social accommodation, state actors and other institutions are also debating the question of how to categorize and treat immigrants. Are we Ethiopian, *ferenji*, or something else altogether? (Or, to repeat the social studies question, "Class, what is Haile?") In the course of our northern travels in particular, I found myself scrutinized under several different frameworks. For example, hotels, churches and museums, most of them state-owned, look to citizenship to determine whether a visitor is entitled to the lower rates generally available to Ethiopians. That definition works well for purposes of differentiating between Ethiopians living in Ethiopia and say, German or Spanish tourists, but it totally excludes the thousands of first generation immigrants who have changed their citizenship for reasons that often have little to do with their identification with Ethiopia. In the cool stone lobby of the government-owned Goha hotel in Gondar, a rather indifferent clerk sniffed that I was not Ethiopian because I did not have an Ethiopian passport. I didn't mind the idea of a different rate for foreigners, or even the proposition that some Ethiopians should pay more, given their greater resources compared to other Ethiopians. But I did mind that someone else had come up with a definition of "Ethiopian" that excluded me. Coincidentally, we checked in just before an Italian couple we had greeted in Axum, and the irony of making no distinction between me and two Italian nationals upset me even more.

The Goha clerk was not moved by my bitter protests, but elsewhere hotel managers and others seemed troubled by a rule that declared me a foreigner—several times I got a "special" twenty-five percent discount, almost, it felt, by way of apology. And in Lalibela, the rule was tossed out in favor of an entirely different paradigm. In that impoverished and isolated town, where my uncle is a frequent visitor and generous employer, I was defined by my affiliation with him. Engineer Tadesse's niece? Of course I was Ethiopian. End of inquiry.

The state-owned Ethiopian Airlines, by contrast, defined Ethiopian by looking to a passenger's birthplace (the agents referred to it as "be-dem"—or "by blood"). Unlike citizenship, this definition takes in the majority of Ethiopians outside Ethiopia, most of whom are first generation. I suspect that the airline adopted this more inclusive policy because it more frequently comes into contact with immigrants, both tourists and those in Ethiopia to pursue business opportunities, and because the price differential is high enough to make immigrants feel and therefore protest the financial bite of exclusion—for example, I paid barely one-third of what Jean paid for our internal tickets. But the policy is still not welcoming of everyone who might feel Ethiopian. Had I been traveling, say, with my younger sister and brother, one of whom was born a few months before we left Ethiopia and the other a few months later, the distinction the airline would have drawn between them would have seemed completely arbitrary.

One of the things my parents asked me to do in Addis Ababa was to deliver a thick stack of translated, notarized assignment documents to the lawyer who had successfully won back title to our house. At the time of our visit, Ethiopia flatly prohibited non-nationals—defined once again as people with foreign citizenship—from owning property.

This rule was the sharpest and most far-reaching exclusion of immigrants I encountered. In our case, it meant that my mother, who has become an American citizen, could not keep her interest in our house; whereas my father, who, despite his deep disdain for Ethiopian governments, has never been able to make the change, could. Like the hotel clerks who gave me the special discounts, our lawyer seemed uncomfortable with the proposition that my mother was not Ethiopian—he apologized twice about the need for the assignment and promised me that once my father's interest was protected, he would look for a way to reinstate my mother's claim. For my parents, the law dampened the thrill of winning back the house and eroded the new tie to their country that the victory had brought. For me, the premise that my mother and father, having shared a relationship to Ethiopia in their forty years of marriage, should now be treated differently by Ethiopia because of steps taken in America, felt wrong and out of balance. Drawing any sort of line between the two of them in matters Ethiopian seemed even less tenable than drawing a line between my younger siblings.

We must not have been the only ones displaced or otherwise troubled by the law. Soon after our trip, the government announced a change in policy in recognition of the fact that "a significant number of foreign nationals of Ethiopian origin wish to strengthen their ties with their country of origin." Henceforth, the government proclaimed, "foreign nationals of Ethiopian origin"—that is, anyone who had once been an Ethiopian national, plus anyone who had at least one parent, grandparent or great-grandparent who was an Ethiopian national—will have the same general economic rights as Ethiopian nationals. (Anyone, that is, except Eritrean nationals. That particular divide apparently remains too recent and raw for such inclusive overtures.) The new law thus harmonizes the treatment of immigrants by introducing a most inclusive definition of Ethiopian. That is, having raised the question of who is Ethiopian, the state has given an answer that represents a major accommodation of immigrants. The next time I travel to Ethiopia, I won't have to argue with hotel clerks about my status; my mother can reclaim her share of our house if she wants to; and both my younger siblings will be recognized as Ethiopians if that is what they want.

I was surprised by these signs of a changing society, but I should not have been. After all, the 1974 revolution, the most significant event of the last thirty years, was at least partly a societal response to Ethiopia's first influential batch of "outsiders," the students Haile Selassie sent abroad in the 1950s and 1960s. These young men (and a few women) returned to Ethiopia transformed into an educated, urban elite who must truly have been at odds with traditional society, strangers in some ways to their own parents, brothers and sisters. I cannot imagine, for example, how my father, who spent eleven years abroad and mastered five foreign languages along the way, could have described to my grandparents the essence of his days in Cairo and Tübingen in the vocabulary of the single language they shared. In time, these students came to make up the core group of university professors and other activists to call for political and social reform; their ideas and, indeed, their very presence brought fundamental change to Ethiopia. The immediate consequence of the revolution, the Derg's rise to power, turned thousands of Ethiopians into political, social and economic refugees and created, for the first time in Ethiopian history, a huge diaspora population that has continued to grow under the TPLF. Now, many of these immigrants have established themselves in their new countries and are beginning to reestablish ties with Ethiopia. In the process, they—or rather, we—have become the impetus for the changes I witnessed. Far from being the lone and lonely outsider I had feared I would be, I am in fact just one of many line-straddlers to press family, friends, strangers and the state to rethink the content of the word "Ethiopian."

So what sort of relationship can I now claim with my old home, twenty-five years after our departure? As I sift through my month in Ethiopia, through the long days with family, through the brief encounters with embassy guards, island monks and curious children, through the meaning I found in Axum, Lalibela and Lake Tana, I find that the answer is not the simple one I had imagined before the trip. The discovery that Ethiopia is interested in making sense of and even accommodating me, that it is willing to consider meeting me at a point somewhere between the country I left and the woman I've since become, presents me with a much more complicated picture.

To start with the old: my trip to Ethiopia affirmed what I have felt since those early days when I relied on my past to define myself in strange new Minnesota. In the summer of 1976, and during the years that followed, I laid claim to Ethiopia for the most elemental reasons of birth and family. I took my association with Ethiopia as a given: a fundamental, if private, relationship that did not need analysis or examination. As I traveled through Ethiopia so many years later, I experienced powerful moments of connection that affirmed this tie, despite the temporal, geographic and cultural distance that had caused me so much concern. The Ethiopian Orthodox Church will never be mine, yet at Narga Selassie I felt as much at peace as I have felt anywhere. The language and people of modern Axum put me off, but the city's remarkable ruins reaffirmed the cultural pride I've carried with me all my life. The trip to Lalibela took me through regions far removed from my own life, yet I responded to the majesty of the Zagwe churches and the beauty of the Lasta mountains with intense and personal pride. Most important, while I have grown away from the family that frames my window onto Ethiopia, its members remain loving and completely accessible to me. My aging grandmother insists on seeing me off at the airport, my aunt Itiyobia offers me a cherished photograph she has carried in her handbag for half a century. Not for the first time, Mimi and Tadesse treat me like the daughter they never had, and every one of them extends his or her affection to the husband who accompanies me. Had I returned to the static society of my imagination, had Ethiopia otherwise not made a single overture towards me, I still would have felt connected through the unconditional embrace of a loving family.

To continue with the new: the trip to Ethiopia taught me that the society is not static, and that the work of belonging does not rest on my shoulders alone. Friends, family, strangers, the state—time again, people and institutions stopped to consider the person I've become and to ask what that person means for societal definitions of woman, of Orthodox, of Ethiopian. And in the process of scrutinizing me and other immigrants against these definitions, the people and institutions asking the questions are themselves changed.

The discovery that Ethiopia can and is changing in response to its outsiders opens the door to an entirely new and unexpected relationship with my old country. Now, I have reason to hope that the conservative, objectionable aspects of Addis Ababa culture that I can never accept might someday fade. I have reason to hope that the Church will preserve a space where I can claim its history and culture despite my lack of faith. I have reason to think that despite a violent departure and thirty years abroad, my family can once again call Ethiopia home, on the strength of ties that begin with ownership of a granite house and continue with broader personal claims to an evolving country. And beyond what I have already seen, I think that I can even dream about the unintended changes that this new class of outsiders, like the students of the 1960s and 1970s, might yet trigger. Perhaps, as immigrants invest in family homes and local enterprises, we will surprise the government with demands for legal protections that level economic playing fields and limit state control. Perhaps assumptions about free speech developed in the West will slowly force the state to loosen its media monopolies, lift restrictions on the independent press and release jailed journalists. Perhaps, in time, our involvement will slowly inch Ethiopia closer to real democratic change.

The discovery allows me to imagine that even I, so distant in so many ways and for so long, can participate as the next chapters of Ethiopian history unfold.

A journey that began with the drama and noise of gunfire and revolution ends with the much quieter sound of doors swinging open again. The knowledge that Ethiopia is not frozen in time makes it possible for me to imagine the nostalgic attachment of childhood evolving into an adult relationship with a beautiful but troubled country. I understand that I and others like me can affect Ethiopia, and I hope that I am up to the responsibility that that implies.

* * *

Jean left Ethiopia before I did, and Tadesse and I took him to the airport to catch his evening flight to Frankfurt. On the way back to the house, my uncle and I drove in silence through the dim nighttime streets until Tadesse suddenly burst out, "Good! He is gone; that is one big headache gone for us. Now our problem is how to finish with the next ten days with you!" I wasn't sure exactly what he meant, but before I could ask the question, he had contradicted himself.

"It will not be long enough, not for you and not for us," he said.

And it wasn't.

ACKNOWLEDGEMENTS

I wish to express my deepest gratitude to my friends Paul Hogan, Pete Aiken, Mel Bissell, Anne Melvin and especially Sipi Bhandari, all of whom read early drafts and offered countless helpful suggestions, and to my husband Jean Manas, without whose love, encouragement and constant challenge to do better I could not have gotten this done at all.

For inspiration, I have had my parents, Getatchew Haile and Misrak Amare Haile, my aunts, Hirut (Mimi) Amare and Martha Amare, and my uncle, Tadesse Haile Selassie.

Glossary

There is no standard method for representing Amharic words, which are written in Ethiopic script, in Roman letters. I have tried to use the most common Roman letter spellings for Amharic words or names that appear often in English. Other words I have tried to represent phonetically.

Ababa: term used to address a father or grandfather.

alicha wat: *wat* that is flavored with mild spices rather than with the widely used *berbere*, a hot red chili pepper.

Amharic (Amarinya): official language of Ethiopia; mother tongue of approximately forty percent of population.

Assab: Red Sea port city located on the southern Eritrean coast.

atakilt: vegetables.

bet/bete: house/house of.

birr: Ethiopian monetary unit, composed of 100 cents. At the time of my trip, the exchange rate was about eight *birr* to one U.S. dollar.

Derg: military junta that deposed Emperor Haile Selassie in 1975. The Derg was composed of perhaps 120 young military officers, none above the rank of major, drawn from the main units of the army, air force, navy, and police.

ferenj/ferenji: term used to describe Westerners.

gari: flatbed cart with an anterior seat for a driver and one or two passengers, usually pulled by a horse or mule.

Ge'ez: the language of Ethiopian Orthodox Church liturgy and scholarly texts. Ge'ez is studied and read but no longer spoken outside church services.

gommen: greens such as spinach, collard greens and kale.

gursha: a bite-size morsel prepared by wrapping *injera* around choice bits of *wat* or *tibs* and then offered to a guest.

habesha: word used to describe Ethiopians (and Eritreans) of the central and northern highlands.

habesha nat! ere aydelechim: "She is *habesha*! No, she isn't!"

Haile Selassie: Emperor of Ethiopia, November 1930 to September 1974.

ighzeryistlign: thank you, literally "may God reward you on my behalf."

injera: flat, crepe-like sour bread made from the grain *tef.*

ishe: okay, alright, used to indicate assent.

jelba: small motorized wooden boats I saw on Lake Tana.

killils: ethnicity-based administrative regions in modern day Federal Republic of Ethiopia. The current government replaced the old province system with *killils* in 1996. There are nine *killils,* each meant to be the geographic home of an ethnic group, plus two chartered cities, Addis Ababa and Dire Dawa.

kitfo: diced raw beef spiced with pepper; similar to steak tartare.

kolo: mixture of dried chickpeas, grains, lightly spiced and salted and eaten as a snack or served with drinks.

Mekele: major town in Tigre province (*killil*).

mels: literally a "homecoming" of the bride, one of many parties thrown by friends and family for newlyweds during the months following the wedding.

Mengistu Haile-Mariam: junior military officer who became chairman of the Derg and was the Ethiopian head of state from 1976 until 1991.

meqdes: the innermost sanctuary of a church, in which a church's *tabot* is stored. Only ordained clergy, bishops, priests and deacons, may enter the *meqdes.*

misir wat: vegetarian *wat* made of lentils.

Missewa: Red Sea port city located on the northern Eritrean coast; also spelled Massawa.

Nazareth: village approximately eighty kilometers from Addis Ababa.

netela: traditional white cotton shawl with decorative embroidered edges, usually worn over matching dress.

Ogaden: the area of southeast Ethiopia bordering Somalia.

Orominya: second most widely spoken language in Ethiopia; mother tongue of approximately forty percent of population.

Red Terror: campaign of terror unleashed by the Derg in

response to the urban guerrilla warfare of the Ethiopian People's Revolutionary Party and later of other leftist civilian opponents of the Derg, such as the All-Ethiopia Socialist Movement, during which thousands of mostly young people were jailed, tortured, and killed. The Red Terror lasted from about February 1977 until early 1978.

shemma: traditional white cotton dress adorned with colorful embroidered hem and neckline, usually worn with a matching shawl or *netela.*

Shoa: central Ethiopian province in pre-1996 Ethiopia. Addis Ababa is in Shoa.

tankwa: traditional papyrus reed canoe still used on Lake Tana.

tef: grain indigenous to Ethiopia, to which its consumption is almost entirely confined. *Tef* flour is used to make *injera,* the traditional form of cereal intake.

tej: mead or sweet wine made of fermented honey.

tenastilign: form of greeting, literally "May He give you health on my behalf."

tibs: cubed beef or lamb sautéed with peppers, onions and spices.

Tigre: northernmost Ethiopian province in pre-1996 Ethiopia.

Tigre People's Liberation Front: also known as the TPLF; the group of guerrillas who fought, defeated and replaced the Derg in 1991 and that, reconstituted as the Ethiopian People's Revolutionary Democratic Front, or EPRPF, has ruled Ethiopia ever since.

Tigrinya: Ethiopian language spoken by approximately six percent of population. Tigrinya, like Amharic, is a Semitic language that is derived from Ge'ez. Tigrinya is also the official language of Eritrea.

tukul: small, round, thatched-roof hut.

Tye: literally, "sister," term of endearment used to address aunts, older sisters and cousins and close female family friends.

wat: thick traditional stews that are made with meat, chicken, lamb or vegetables and flavored with a variety of spices such as curry, pepper and turmeric. *Wat* is eaten with *injera*, which is torn into small pieces and wrapped around morsels. The traditional meal is not eaten with utensils.

wey ye ferenj neger: ah, the ways of foreigners!

Wollo: province in pre-1996 Ethiopia, located just north of Shoa. Wollo is home to Lalibela and the Lasta mountains.

Zagwe: dynasty of monarchs who overthrew the Axumite dynasty in the ninth century and ruled Ethiopia from Lalibela until 1270 A.D.

zebenya: guard, usually of a residential or commercial compound.

zemecha: literally "campaign," in the military sense. Used to denote the Derg's Development Through Cooperation Campaign, which was launched as part of its initial land reform in 1975. Early implementation included the conscription of university and secondary school students who were sent to the countryside to promote literacy and explain the socialist revolution, including land reform, to peasants.